Baz Luhrmann: Interviews

Conversations with Filmmakers Series
Gerald Peary, General Editor

Baz Luhrmann

INTERVIEWS

Edited by Tom Ryan

University Press of Mississippi / Jackson

www.upress.state.ms.us

The University Press of Mississippi is a member
of the Association of American University Presses.

Copyright © 2014 by University Press of Mississippi
All rights reserved
Manufactured in the United States of America

First printing 2014
∞
Library of Congress Cataloging-in-Publication Data

Luhrmann, Baz.
  Baz Luhrmann: interviews / edited by Tom Ryan.
    pages cm. — (Conversations with filmmakers series)
  Includes bibliographical references and index.
  Includes filmography.
    ISBN 978-1-62846-149-7 (cloth : alk. paper) — ISBN 978-1-62846-150-3 (ebook) 1.
Luhrmann, Baz—Interviews. 2. Motion picture producers and directors—Australia—
Interviews. I. Ryan, Tom. II. Title.
  PN1998.3.L839A3 2014
  791.43092'33092—dc23   2014014369

British Library Cataloging-in-Publication Data available

Contents

Introduction

"The magic of Baz is that he's one of those rare beings who can convince others the impossible can be possible." Craig Pearce[1]

"When you're the subject of something, you know, it's very difficult. I'm in the business of making stories about subjects, people. I'm in the character analysis business. My own character has always been a bit elusive to me. I'm also a storyteller . . . I'll tell you anything as long as it doesn't hurt someone else." Baz Luhrmann[2]

"Maybe I'm sick of dancing somebody else's steps all of the time." Scott (Paul Mercurio) in *Strictly Ballroom* [1993]

"We're gonna Baz the shit out of it." Sean (Patrick Brammall) in episode 4 of the Australian TV comedy series *A Moody Christmas* [2012], in reference to the creative approach he and his collaborators are planning to take to the production of a Nativity play.

Chronologically ordered, the interviews in this book trace the arc of Baz Luhrmann's career so far, taking us from the genesis of his 1993 film, *Strictly Ballroom*, based on the original thirty-minute theatrical production, through to the preparations for the 2014 stage version of *Strictly Ballroom*, which is in turn adapted from the film, and his plans for future projects. Along the way, the book also takes a sidelong glance at his eclectic output beyond his feature films, seeking insights there into both his work as a whole and his working methods.

The most obvious point to make about this portrait of an artist who loves to put on a show, preferably a musical, is that it has all the hallmarks of a star-is-born saga. The boy who ran away from home. The escape from the constraints of smalltown Australia to the excitements of the Big City. The search for a new direction: something full of color and style. His struggle to make a success of himself. The determination to do things his way and the refusal to bend to the dictates of others or back off in the face of public disapproval. The big hit that launched his career on a global scale. The discovery of a soul-mate. The international recognition that followed.

But alongside the success story is another one. It has to do with the insecurities that have plagued him over the years, fears of failure that dog not only those who embark on careers in the arts and show business but also, perhaps, all of us. From Luhrmann's public protestations, it's clear that these self-doubts have been exacerbated by the treatment meted out to his work—indeed to him—by much of "the middle-class, middle-aged, white-skinned film establishment,"[3] and by others too. He divides people, critics and audiences, but not those who've worked with him, the team he's built up around himself.

The antipathy of those who believe he hasn't earned the plaudits others have heaped upon him or the escalating budgets he's been able to extract from accommodating studios seems to have been fuelled by a resentment that's hard to explain.[4] Perhaps it's to do with "the tall poppy" syndrome, the desire to cut down to size people who are seen to have grown too big for their boots. He's the small-town boy who now lists among his friends and acquaintances an abundance of Big Names from the arts and showbiz worlds, figures as disparate as Elton (John), Kenny (Branagh), Francis (Ford Coppola), and Kim (Kardashian). Who does he think he is?

Perhaps what is perceived as his constant self-promotion is responsible: heavily involved in the marketing of his films, he seems to embrace the attention of all strands of the media with the same intensity that they bring to him. Talk about a show off! Or perhaps the hostility is a consequence of his commitment to realms of the arts and entertainment worlds—musicals, opera, fashion, and music—that are notoriously resistant to critical explication. Whatever the source, though, it's frequently vicious.

In his review of *The Great Gatsby*, Peter Bradshaw of the *Guardian* wielded his wit like a weapon, describing Luhrmann as "a man who can't see a nuance without calling security for it to be thrown off his set."[5] An Australian gossip columnist was equally scathing in his sarcastic dismissal of the filmmaker's preparation for the film. He writes, "The idea to take on the job of bringing a new version of *Gatsby* to the big screen did not come to the fifty-year-old *Strictly Ballroom* and *Australia* visionary after reading Fitzgerald's unforgettable rumination on romance, tragedy, and the American dream but while quaffing red wine and listening to a *Gatsby* audio book on the Trans-Siberian Railway in 2004."[6] And in his review of the film for the *New Yorker*, David Denby went into brutal, full-on assault mode charging that "Luhrmann's vulgarity is designed to win over the young audience, and it suggests that he's less a filmmaker than a music-video director with endless resources and a stunning absence of taste."[7] He was similarly hostile to *Australia*.

For every excited celebration of Luhrmann's work, there'll be a hostile denunciation. In an illuminating symposium published in 1998 by *Cineaste* magazine[8]—which includes contributions by Luhrmann, included in this volume—British director Oliver Parker, who brought *Othello* to the screen in 1995, describes *Romeo + Juliet* as "passionate and poignant and hugely accessible." On the other hand, though, Franco Zeffirelli, who broke new ground with his own screen adaptation of *Romeo and Juliet* in 1968 (as well as making *The Taming of the Shrew* the previous year), was contemptuous of it. "The Luhrmann film didn't update the play," he accuses. "It just made a big joke of it. But apparently the pseudo-culture of young people today wouldn't have digested the play unless you dressed it up that way, with all those fun and games."

Marcia Langton, a descendant of the Yiman and Bidjara nations and professor of Australian Indigenous Studies at the University of Melbourne, enthusiastically sang the praises of Luhrmann's *Australia*, acclaiming it as "a myth of national origin that is disturbing, thrilling, heartbreaking, hilarious, and touching."[9] Shortly afterwards, Germaine Greer took her to task for missing the point that "myths are by definition untrue," and arguing that, in his "fatuous plot," "the only history Luhrmann seems to care about is the history of movies."[10]

The director is right when he observes, with a resigned shrug, "My negatives aren't just ordinary negatives. They're 'You Offend Me' negatives. 'You have offended cinema.' It's personal."[11] Like all of us, he wants to be taken seriously. He knows his film history, draws upon it adventurously and would like those who disapprove of his endeavours to at least examine them seriously before passing judgement. Yet it's rare to find any disapproving commentary about his work that goes far beyond the usual easy putdown-adjectives: "flashy," "indulgent," "excessive," "unsubtle," "superficial," "crass," and so on.

In the introduction to her book about him, Pam Cook perceptively touches on areas for further discussion.[12] "On an aesthetic level, all his films conjure up their settings as imaginary dreamscapes that transcend time and place," she contends. Then, pondering what she describes as "his aesthetic of artifice," she adds, "The skill and the craftsmanship involved are made visible through a painterly technique that draws attention to technological processes rather than naturalising them in the interests of realism." She further notes that "from research stage to the final product, Luhrmann and [production and costume designer and wife Catherine] Martin's work is grounded in pastiche,"[13] going on to note that *Strictly Ballroom*'s "underlying principle is one of appropriation rather than reverence,"[14] and, in the process, pointing to the modus operandi that has been in evidence throughout Luhrmann's career.

But his work generally remains an oeuvre calling out for in-depth analysis: both thematically and stylistically, there's an irresistible consistency to it. All of his films are about characters who come from different cultural backgrounds, are drawn together because of that, or despite it, and who either end up together or are driven apart by forces seemingly beyond their control. Scott and Fran in *Strictly Ballroom*. Romeo and Juliet. Christian and Satine in *Moulin Rouge!* Lady Sarah Ashley and the Drover With No Name in *Australia*. Gatsby and Daisy.

At the same time, the impulse to community and the need to belong drive them all, even as they struggle with the shackles of conformity that their circumstances impose on them. Luhrmann's films are preoccupied with how rigid attachments to class and cultural difference become causes of social breakdown, as destructive to the workings of a society as they are to the aspirations of its citizens. Given this, it would be seriously misguided to regard the very decorative trappings of Luhrmann's style and his films' visual exuberance as ends rather than means.

A musical about multiculturalism, *Strictly Ballroom* tells a mythic tale about David and Goliath and about what an oppressive, white, patriarchal Australia tied to its traditions has to learn from other cultures and from another generation less fixed in its ways. Its implications also take it far beyond Australia's shores. As Luhrmann tells Peter Brunette during their conversation about the film's Cold War overtones, "To me, the film is not about ballroom dancing. It's about overcoming oppression, whatever nature that oppression takes."

Conceived in the context of a very public debate about the need for an official national reconciliation between white Australia and the indigenous owners of the land, *Australia* is Luhrmann's most overtly political film to date. It wastes no time getting to the point as an opening scroll points to the suffering inflicted on those who have become known as "the stolen generation" and whose fate continues to cast a shadow across the nation. These are the children of Australian Aboriginal people and Torres Strait islanders who, in line with a shameful official government policy, were removed—and, according to newspaper reports, continue to be removed—from their parents and placed in "state care."[15]

What follows, however, gradually unfolds into an irrepressibly optimistic yarn about the movement of Australian history towards a new kind of community. This utopian idyll is, finally, drawn together by the stories the characters tell to and hear from each other. And by the story Luhrmann is telling us. It's not by chance that the narrator, Nullah (Brandon Walters), the film's dominant voice, is one of the forgotten people, a half-caste who describes himself as "a creamy, a no-one" and who needs to have his story heard.

Luhrmann's approach from the beginning of his career has been an immersive one, the sheer visual exuberance of his films designed to grab our attention and keep it, to sweep us into the world he's creating and stop us from looking away. John Lahr appropriately refers to him in his eloquent portrait-by-interview as "the entrepreneur of astonishment." Light and color, gracefully choreographed camera moves and rapid-fire editing combine to create a state of bedazzlement in the viewer. The choice of 3D to shoot *The Great Gatsby* is a perfectly logical consequence of this.

In Peter Malone's interview with him, Luhrmann spells out where his priorities lie. Malone asks, "Your sets? Do you ever think, 'This is just too much? This is overwhelming?'" Luhrmann replies with a question: "Do you mean too much in terms of its effectiveness in the storytelling, or just incredibly decadent?" The requested clarification shows that Luhrmann's appreciation of what might constitute "excess" is considerably more sophisticated than his detractors' regular throwaway use of the term in relation to his work.

His methods have nothing to do with the pursuit of any kind of realism. But, at the same time, they're firmly rooted in a concern with the workings of the real world. As Ray Pride notes in his introduction to his interview with the director, "Luhrmann is fixed on attaining the authentic through the inauthentic." Or, as Luhrmann himself puts it, he's interested in creating "a real artificiality" rather than "an artificial reality."[16]

He is nothing if not famous for his perfectionism and his exhaustive attention to detail (Martin's contributions to the visual design of his films can't be underestimated). As illustrated by the six-month postponement of the release date for *The Great Gatsby*—from Christmas 2012 to mid-2013—he has trouble with deadlines. As he confesses to Terry Keefe in the interview about his production of *La Boheme*, "I take forever to do stuff."

Reports from insiders and outsiders, who find themselves privy to his working methods, repeatedly testify to his hands-on approach to his work and a determination to make the films bearing his name look exactly the way he wants them to. In the Malone interview, he explains why: "The act of making must make your life rich. It's got to be interesting and fulfilling and educational and take you on a journey."

All of the interviews contained within this book explicitly or implicitly find a direct connection between the way Luhrmann presents himself and his work. His flamboyance, his eclecticism, and his layered approach to conversation, filled with asides-within-asides, are all recurring features. A conversation with Baz is analogous to watching one of his films: you're never sure where exactly they're likely to go next. All you know is that they're going to go there with a flourish.

He's a showman, through and through. Observations by interviewers in this book about how he talks up a storm are apposite. Elsie Walker refers to his "multi-clause, rapid-fire, and multi-directional speaking rhythm." Lahr reflects on how he "bushwhacks his way through a tangle of articulation to a new thought." Pride observes that "Luhrmann is one of the fastest talkers I've ever encountered, and is willing to let his thoughts tumble over each other in his clipped, sometimes nasal speech," also referring (in a personal correspondence, quoted with permission) to "Baz's breathless antipodean tumult."

Taken together, these interviews indicate that Luhrmann is never prepared simply to go through the motions. During my encounter with him, at one point he leapt to his feet to act out a scene, later directing me to move around the room cupping his hands in the shape of a viewfinder so that I'd better understand how he wanted the 3D to work in the Plaza suite scene in *The Great Gatsby*.

The window in the hotel room where that interview was conducted looked out over Sydney Harbor and the Opera House, and I suspect much time was spent ensuring that the setting was just right. On the morning I arrived in Sydney to be one of a steady stream of interviewers, I received word that the location had been changed from the city's Tiffany & Co. store to the Park Hyatt, as if he couldn't quite make up his mind about which location would create a more striking impression.

Of course, there was nothing anyone could do about the rain, a recurring problem for him it would seem. "If you ever need your garden watered," he told me as I entered the room, "just invite me over." The previous evening, he'd walked the red carpet for the Australian launch of *The Great Gatsby* under an umbrella, although the downpour hadn't dampened his spirits in the slightest.

Such is his way of dealing with the world that I suspect that nothing could. "Everywhere I go, it seems that it decides to rain," he said, referring to the film's mid-summer opening of the Cannes Film Festival on the other side of the world a couple of weeks earlier. "And then there was the time that we did a launch of *Australia* in the outback, where it hadn't rained for ten years, and, of course, it poured. Then there was the torrential downpour that delayed us on *Gatsby*. . . ."

Friendly and forthright, Luhrmann took our interview to places I'd never expected it to go, and both commanded and won my attention throughout. And what at times had begun to seem like a scattergun approach to conversation usually drew the various volleys together on its way back to the point that was its target in the first place.

What matters to him above all else is the work. And it would appear that Luhrmann is either drawn to a project because he's able to find autobiographical elements in it or finds them emerging from the material as he's working on it. For example, in her interview regarding *Strictly Ballroom*, Ruth Hessey proposes that "there's more than a skerrick of Fran [Tara Morice] in Luhrmann," while others have linked the endeavours by Scott (Paul Mercurio) in the same film with Luhrmann's struggle to have his voice heard at Australia's National Institute of Dramatic Art (NIDA). Lahr also sees the entire film itself as a metaphor for, among other things, the director's increasing sense of "creative oppression" there.

In *Moulin Rouge!* one can argue that Luhrmann the filmmaker is not only unreservedly empathising with Christian (Ewan McGregor), the poet-lover, as he tells us his sad tale of lost love, but also casting himself as one of those contemptuously referred to by the very stupid and very wealthy Duke (Richard Roxburgh) as "underworld showfolk."

In the scene where he's making his pitch to the Duke to persuade him to back the show that he and his friends are planning to produce, one even gets the sense that he's cheekily biting the studio hand that's been feeding him. The dim-witted Duke tries to make it clear that he's no fool, that they're not going to put one over on him: "If I'm to invest, I'll need to know the story," he pompously declares. Christian's reply simultaneously informs and mocks him: "Well, it's about love overcoming all obstacles . . . and there's a courtesan. . . ."

Certainly one could never describe Luhrmann as a director for hire. The passionate concern for the plight of the young lovers in *Romeo + Juliet* and for the sense of displacement that defines Nullah, the narrator in *Australia*, suggests that both films are projects close to his heart. The same applies to *Elsa Schiaparelli and Miuccia Prada: Impossible Conversations*, the eight short films he made for the Metropolitan Museum's

Spring 2012 Costume Institute exhibition in New York (and accessible on YouTube). Judy Davis is Schiaparelli with Prada (a collaborator on *The Great Gatsby*) playing herself. The two women converse about fashion and life. Schiaparelli talks about running away from home to pursue her art, as Luhrmann has said in some interviews that he did. Prada (in the part called *Naif Chic*) declares her commitment to discovering the truth through excess. "When I'm uncertain," she says, "I push even more. Because the only way to make something reasonable out of something that is completely, maybe, wrong, is really to push so much that eventually, it is in excess and eventually says the truth of what I'm thinking."

And, as many commentators have observed, there's also more than a skerrick of Gatsby in Luhrmann too: the changed name, the different stories in circulation about his personal history, the refashioning of a mansion to enable him to achieve his dreams, the liking for putting on a show. As David Edelstein writes in his review of *The Great Gatsby* in *New York*, "Luhrmann throws money at the screen in a way that is positively Gatsby-like. . . ."[17]

His involvement in his work doesn't come to an end when the film is in the can. He's not only the man behind the camera and in the editing room (and occasionally on-screen), but he's also the spruiker on the street trying to persuade you to part with your money. He's hands-on; he wants to make sure that everything's done right. He is, if you like, a control freak. Lahr puts it slightly differently: "Part Barnum and part Diaghilev, Luhrmann is also something of an imperialist," he says. "He controls the look of every poster, every sign, every piece of information connected to each of his shows, because, as he says, 'You're already in the show, even before you've bought a ticket.'" But, as the conversations in this book illustrate, the fact that he does interviews because he's got something to sell doesn't mean he doesn't have anything interesting to say.

Who is Baz Luhrmann then? In her book, Cook writes of how he projects himself as a "buccaneering adventurer,"[18] perhaps with Errol Flynn as his swashbuckling model. I think the answer that emerges from the interviews that follow also suggests that he knows very well that he's in the business of putting on a show, not just in his films and other works but in the public face that he presents to the world. He's a self-created enigma, and he warns us not to take everything he says about himself as the gospel truth. As he tells Lahr, "I was mythologizing my own existence from the age of ten." And his interviews are littered with contradictions, gaps, throwaway but revealing bits and pieces, elements that have as much to do with myth-making as truth-telling, flavoured by real or imagined encounters with the rich, famous, and fashionable.

However, the more important question in my view is: what are we to make of Luhrmann's work? The probings of the interviewers here, who come to it from a wide range of vantage points, and Luhrmann's commitment to responding to them in detail and at length construct a strong case for why it matters.

Thanks are due to many people, beginning with the contributors to this volume. My dear friend Barry White also provided invaluable technical assistance and regular advice. The ever-helpful staff at the Australian Film Institute Library in Melbourne assisted me with their time and their invaluable filing system for tracking down interviews, and three significant others provided counsel and/or recommended reading along the way: Sharon Krum, Brian McFarlane, and Alan Finney. Most of all, though, I'm forever grateful to my wonderful girls, wife Debi Enker and daughter Madeleine Ryan, for their encouragement, support, and wise counsel over the eighteen months or so it took to compile this book and their patience as I laid siege to the Luhrmann citadel. Unfortunately the filmmaker declined to make himself available for interview outside the parameters of PR promotions for his productions.

TR

Notes

1. *UK Telegraph*, May 13, 2013.

2. Author's interview with Baz Luhrmann, May 23, 2013.

3. Ibid.

4. *Strictly Ballroom*: $3 million; *Romeo + Juliet*: $15 million; *Moulin Rouge!*: $52 million; *Australia*: $78 million; *The Great Gatsby*: $190 million (all amounts approximate and in US dollars).

5. Peter Bradshaw, *Guardian* (UK), May 14, 2014.

6. Luke Buckmaster, *Crikey* (Australia), April 30, 2013.

7. David Denby, *New Yorker*, May 13, 2013.

8. *Cineaste* 24, no. 1 (December 1998): 48–55.

9. Marcia Langton, "Faraway Downs Fantasy Resonates Close to Home," *Sunday Age* (Melbourne), November 23, 2008.

10. Germaine Greer, "Strictly Fanciful," *The Age*, December 17, 2008.

11. Op. cit., author's interview with Baz Luhrmann.

12. Pam Cook, *Baz Luhrmann*, 2–3.

13. Ibid., 22.

14. Ibid., 47.

15. Vince Chadwick, "Nation Risks a New Stolen Generation, Leaders Warn," *The Age*, June 15, 2013.

16. *Moulin Rouge*, DVD extras.

17. David Edelstein, "Why I Sort of Liked *The Great Gatsby*," *New York*, May 7, 2013.

18. Cook, op. cit., 5.</notes>

Chronology

1962	Born Mark Anthony Luhrmann on September 17, 1962, in Sydney, New South Wales, on the back seat of a car on its way to hospital. Parents Leonard and Barbara Luhrmann.
1962–74	Grew up in Herons Creek, a small country town on the north coast of New South Wales. His father ran a petrol station there and managed a cinema at nearby Laurieton. After his parents' divorce in 1974, he initially stayed with his father but ended up living in Sydney with his mother.
1975–76	Student at St. Joseph's Hasting Regional School and the Balgowlah Boys Campus.
1977–79	Leaves Herons Creek. Attends a Catholic boys' high school and Narrabeen Sports High School, where he meets future collaborator Craig Pearce.
1979	Appears in a school production of *Guys and Dolls* as Sky Masterson with Pearce as Nathan Detroit. Officially changes his name to Bazmark.
1980	Applies unsuccessfully for entry into the National Institute of Dramatic Art (NIDA).
1981–82	Makes his film debut in John Duigan's *Winter of Our Dreams*. Co-directs and acts in *Kids of the Cross*. Has a small role in *The Dark Room*. Appears in six episodes of the long-running Australian TV series *A Country Practice*. Forms The Bond, a theatre company.
1983	After reauditioning for NIDA, he is accepted and begins the three-year acting course there. His work at the Institute includes August Strindberg's *The Ghost Sonata*.
1984	Devises and directs the first production of *Strictly Ballroom* at NIDA, which runs for around thirty minutes. He also plays the role of Ross Pierce with Catherine McClements as his wife, Barbara.
1985	Chosen to work as a production assistant on Peter Brook's

production of *The Mahabharata* as part of Australia's bicentennial celebrations. Graduates from NIDA.

1986   He is invited to stage *Strictly Ballroom* at the World Youth Theatre Festival in Bratislava, the capital of Slovakia. He revises the script with Craig Pearce and the production wins awards for Best Production and Best Director.

1987   Directs the historical musical play *Crocodile Creek*, set and performed in the Queensland goldfields with music by Felix Meagher and a multi-national cast.

1988   Under the auspices of the Sydney Theatre Company, he establishes the Six Years Old Company, based at the Wharf Theatre in Sydney. Other members include McClements, Pearce, production designer and future wife Catherine Martin, set designer Bill Marron, and costume designer Angus Strathie. Further productions of *Strictly Ballroom* are performed at the Wharf Theatre in Sydney and at the World Expo in Brisbane. The company's other productions include *Haircut*, a revision of *Hair*.

1989   As the artistic director of the Ra Project for the Australian Opera, he stages the opera *Lake Lost* with composer Felix Meagher. With Martin, he produces *Dance Hall* at the Sydney Town Hall. The "event" recreates a 1940s dance-hall and invites those in attendance to relive the night celebrating the end of World War II.

1990   His stage version of Giacomo Puccini's *La Boheme* opens at the Sydney Opera House on July 28, produced for the Australian Opera with sets and costumes by Martin and Marron. It was subsequently revived there in 1993 and 1996. The 1993 production, directed for the Australian Broadcasting Commission by Geoffrey Nottage, is available on DVD.

1992   *Strictly Ballroom* premieres at the Cannes Film Festival in May, winning the Prix de la jeunesse and a special mention for the Camera d'Or. 20th Century Fox signs Luhrmann to a three-year first-look deal.

1993   His Hindu-styled production of Benjamin Britten's version of *A Midsummer Night's Dream*, set in colonial India, is performed for the Australian Opera in Sydney and Melbourne. He and Martin work with the Australian Labor Party on the Keating government's re-election campaign.

1994   With Martin and Marron, he is a guest editor for the January issue of *Vogue Australia*. His *A Midsummer Night's Dream* wins the Critics' Prize at the Edinburgh Festival.

1996   *William Shakespeare's Romeo + Juliet* is released.

1997   Marries Martin on January 26 (Australia Day and her birthday) at a registry office, the reception held at the Sydney Opera House. "We built a church on the stage, and 'L'Amour' was at the back of the church. . . . It was actually fantastic. You wouldn't believe it, but with all of our experience with stage management, the bride was incredibly late." He and Martin co-found their production company, Bazmark Inq., based in Darlinghurst in Sydney in a mansion they dub The House of Iona. The CD *Something for Everybody* is released, produced by Luhrmann. A track released from it, "Everybody's Free (To Wear Sunscreen)," subsequently goes to the top of the charts in the UK.

1998   Luhrmann and Martin produce designer Collette Dinnigan's 1998 Autumn/Winter Collection at the Louvre in Paris. An ongoing production deal is confirmed with Fox on May 2, Bazmark Inq. devising a backlot area at the Fox Studios in Sydney, which opened on the same day.

2001   Luhrmann is awarded the Australian Centenary Medal in the 2001 Queen's New Year's Honours List for his services to Australian society in film direction and production. His father dies. *Moulin Rouge!* is released, dedicated to his memory.

2002   After a six week sell-out run at San Francisco's Curran Theatre, Luhrmann's production of *La Boheme* opens on Broadway on December 8, running for 228 performances and eventually earning seven Tony nominations, including Best Revival of a Musical and Best Director for Luhrmann, as well as a win for his wife, scenic designer Catherine Martin.

2003   Luhrmann commences pre-production on *Alexander the Great*, the first of what is projected as a trilogy of historical epics. It is set to star Leonardo DiCaprio and Nicole Kidman, with shooting planned to commence in early 2004 on a reported budget of around $US160 million. In November, the project is put on hold, where it remains. On October 10, in Sydney, Luhrmann and Martin's first child, Lillian Amanda, is born.

2004   Luhrmann's production of *La Boheme* opens in Los Angeles at the Ahmanson Theater on January 9. In November, his ad for

	Chanel, *No. 5 The Film*, first appears on TV around the world. He involves himself in mentoring work on the production of the British TV program *My Shakespeare*.
2005	On June 8, in Sydney, Luhrmann and Martin's second child, William Alexander, is born.
2006	*Australia* goes into pre-production, Russell Crowe apparently having been dumped from the project. "[My reps] did not disengage, Baz and Fox did," he told the *Sydney Morning Herald*. "It was hard pinning him down. Every time I was ready, Russell was in something else," Luhrmann told the *Guardian*.
2008	*Australia* is released in November.
2009	For the 81st Academy Awards ceremony, he produces a number celebrating musicals and featuring Hugh Jackman, Beyonce, Zac Efron, Vanessa Hudgens, Dominic Cooper, and Amanda Seyfried. In September, he appears as a guest judge on *Dancing with the Stars* (US).
2010	He goes to India with painter Vincent Fantauzzo on a "ten-day personal peace mission" in January, following assaults on Indian students in Australia. The pair create artworks on the walls of hotels and in streets. Again with Fantauzzo, he showcases work at the Hong Kong International Art Fair from May 26 to May 30: a portrait of Indian actor, Amitabh Bachchan, and a multi-media installation entitled "The Creek, 1977." UK writer Pam Cook's *Baz Luhrmann* is published, the first book-length study of his career.
2012	Donating his services to New York's Metropolitan Museum of Art, he premieres eight short films under the umbrella title of *Elsa Schiaparelli and Miuccia Prada: Impossible Conversations* as part of the Metropolitan Museum's Spring 2012 Costume Institute exhibition in New York from May 10 to August 19. Luhrmann was also creative consultant for the exhibition. He and Martin move to downtown New York with their family.
2013	Shot in 3-D at Fox Studios in Sydney, but made for Warner Bros. and Roadshow pictures, *The Great Gatsby* opens in the US on May 10 and premieres on the opening night of the Cannes Film Festival.
2014	A new stage production of *Strictly Ballroom* premieres in March at the Lyric Theatre in Sydney.

Filmography

STRICTLY BALLROOM (1992)
Produced by M and A Film Corporation
Producer: Tristram Miall
Director: **Baz Luhrmann**
Screenplay: **Baz Luhrmann** and Craig Pearce from a screenplay by
Baz Luhrmann and Andrew Bovell
Cinematography: Steve Mason
Editing: Jill Bilcock
Production Design: Catherine Martin
Art Direction: Martin Brown
Costume Design: Angus Strathie
Choreography: John "Cha Cha" O'Connell
Original Music: David Hirschfelder
Cast: Paul Mercurio (Scott Hastings), Tara Morice (Fran), Bill Hunter
(Barry Fife), Pat Thompson (Shirley Hastings), Barry Otto (Doug Hast-
ings), Antonio Vargas (Rico), Armonia Benedito (Ya Ya), Gia Carides (Liz
Holt), Peter Whitford (Les Kendall), John Hannan (Ken Railings), Sonya
Kruger (Tina Sparkle), Kris McQuade (Charm Leachman), Pip Mushin
(Wayne Burns), Leonie Crane (Vanessa Cronin)
35mm, color, 94 minutes

WILLIAM SHAKESPEARE'S ROMEO + JULIET (1996)
Produced by 20th Century Fox
Producers: **Baz Luhrmann**, Martin Brown, and Gabriella Martinelli
Director: **Baz Luhrmann**
Screenplay: Craig Pearce and **Baz Luhrmann** from the play by Wil-
liam Shakespeare
Cinematography: Donald M. McAlpine
Editing: Jill Bilcock
Production Design: Catherine Martin

Art Direction: Doug Hardwick
Costume Design: Kym Barrett
Choreography: John "Cha Cha" O'Connell
Original Music: Nellee Hooper
Cast: Leonardo DiCaprio (Romeo), Claire Danes (Juliet), John Leguizamo (Tybalt), Harold Perrineau (Mercutio), Miriam Margolyes (The Nurse), Pete Postlethwaite (Friar Laurence), Paul Sorvino (Fulgencio Capulet), Brian Dennehy (Ted Montague), Paul Rudd (Dave Paris), Vondie Curtis-Hall (Captain Prince)
35mm, color, 120 minutes

MOULIN ROUGE! (2001)
Produced by 20th Century Fox
Producers: **Baz Luhrmann**, Fred Barron, and Martin Brown
Director: **Baz Luhrmann**
Screenplay: **Baz Luhrmann** and Craig Pearce
Cinematography: Donald M. McAlpine
Editing: Jill Bilcock
Production Design: Catherine Martin
Art Direction: Doug Hardwick
Costume Design: Catherine Martin and Angus Strathie
Choreography: John "Cha Cha" O'Connell
Original Music: Craig Armstrong
Cast: Nicole Kidman (Satine), Ewan McGregor (Christian), John Leguizamo (Toulouse-Lautrec), Jim Broadbent (Harold Zidler), Richard Roxburgh (The Duke), Garry McDonald (The Doctor), David Wenham (Audrey), Kylie Minogue (Green Fairy), Kerry Walker (Marie), Christine Anu (Arabia)
35mm, color, 123 minutes

AUSTRALIA (2008)
Produced by 20th Century Fox
Producers: G. Mac Brown, Catherine Knapman, and **Baz Luhrmann**
Director: **Baz Luhrmann**
Screenplay: Stuart Beattie, **Baz Luhrmann**, Ronald Harwood, and Richard Flanagan from a story by **Baz Luhrmann**
Cinematography: Mandy Walker
Editing: Dodie Dawn and Michael McCusker
Production Design: Catherine Martin
Art Direction: Ian Gracie and Karen Murphy

Costume Design: Catherine Martin
Original Music: David Hirschfelder
Cast: Nicole Kidman (Lady Sarah Ashley), Hugh Jackman (Drover), Brandon Walters (Nullah), David Wenham (Neil Fletcher), David Gulpilil (King George), Bryan Brown (King Carney), Ben Mendelsohn (Captain Dutton), Ray Barrett (Ramsden), Bill Hunter (Skipper), Essie Davis (Cath Carney), Sandy Gore (Gloria Carney), John Jarratt (Sergeant)
35mm, color, 164 minutes

THE GREAT GATSBY (2013)
Produced by Warner Bros.
Producers: Lucy Fisher, Catherine Knapman, **Baz Luhrmann**, Catherine Martin, and Douglas Wick
Director: **Baz Luhrmann**
Screenplay: **Baz Luhrmann** and Craig Pearce, based on the novel by F. Scott Fitzgerald
Cinematography: Simon Duggan
Editing: Jason Ballantine, Jonathan Redmond, and Matt Villa
Production Design: Catherine Martin
Art Direction: Damien Drew, Ian Gracie, and Michael Turner
Costume Design: Catherine Martin
Original Music: Craig Armstrong
Cast: Leonardo DiCaprio (Jay Gatsby), Cary Mulligan (Daisy Buchanan), Isla Fisher (Myrtle Wilson), Tobey Maguire (Nick Carraway), Joel Edgerton (Tom Buchanan), Elizabeth Debicki (Jordan Fraser), Jason Clarke (George Wilson), Callan McAuliffe (young Jay Gatsby), Adelaide Clemens (Catherine)
3D, color, 143 minutes

Music Clips

BEAT ME DADDY, EIGHT TO THE BAR (1987)
by Ignatius Jones, Pardon Me Boys
Director: **Baz Luhrmann**

LOVE IS IN THE AIR (1992)
by John Paul Young
Director: **Baz Luhrmann**

TIME AFTER TIME (1992)
by Tara Morice
Director: **Baz Luhrmann**

YOUNG HEARTS RUN FREE (1996)
by Harold Perrineau
Director: **Baz Luhrmann**

KISSING YOU (1996)
by Des'ree
Director: **Baz Luhrmann**

NOW UNTIL THE BREAK OF DAY (1997)
by Christine Anu, David Hobson, Royce Doherty, and the Café at the
Gates of Salvation Gospel Choir
Director: **Baz Luhrmann**

LADY MARMALADE (2001)
by Christine Anu, Lil'Kim, Mya, and Pink
Director: **Baz Luhrmann**

ONE DAY I'LL FLY AWAY (2001)
by Nicole Kidman
Director: **Baz Luhrmann**

COME WHAT MAY (2001)
by Ewan McGregor and Nicole Kidman
Director: **Baz Luhrmann**

Commercial

NO. 5 THE FILM (2004)
Producer, Writer, Director: **Baz Luhrmann**
Production Design: Catherine Martin
Costume Design: Karl Lagerfeld and Catherine Martin
Cinematography: Mandy Walker
Editing: Daniel Schwarze
Music: Debussy's *Clair de Lune*, performed by the Sydney Symphony
Orchestra, conducted by Craig Armstrong

Cast: Nicole Kidman, Rodrigo Santoro
3 minutes (although there have been reported longer and shorter screenings)

Short Films

ELSA SCHIAPARELLI AND MIUCCIA PRADA: IMPOSSIBLE CONVERSATIONS (2012)
Director: **Baz Luhrmann**
Additional Dialogue: **Baz Luhrmann**, Andrew Bolton, Schuyler Weiss, and Sam Bromell (adapted from the writings of Elsa Schiaparelli)
Production and Costume Design: Catherine Martin
Producers: Anton Monsted and Schuyler Weiss
Cinematography: Josh Rothstein and Evan Papageorgiou
Editing: Jeremy Kotin
Cast: Judy Davis (as Elsa Schiaparelli) and Miuccia Prada (as herself)
2½ minutes

WAIST UP/WAIST DOWN (2012)
Director: **Baz Luhrmann**
Additional Dialogue: **Baz Luhrmann**, Andrew Bolton, Schuyler Weiss, and Sam Bromell (adapted from the writings of Elsa Schiaparelli)
Production and Costume Design: Catherine Martin
Producers: Anton Monsted and Schuyler Weiss
Cinematography: Josh Rothstein and Evan Papageorgiou
Editing: Jeremy Kotin
Cast: Judy Davis (as Elsa Schiaparelli) and Miuccia Prada (as herself)
2 minutes

HARD CHIC (2012)
Director: **Baz Luhrmann**
Additional Dialogue: **Baz Luhrmann**, Andrew Bolton, Schuyler Weiss, and Sam Bromell (adapted from the writings of Elsa Schiaparelli)
Production and Costume Design: Catherine Martin
Producers: Anton Monsted and Schuyler Weiss
Cinematography: Josh Rothstein and Evan Papageorgiou
Editing: Jeremy Kotin
Cast: Judy Davis (as Elsa Schiaparelli) and Miuccia Prada (as herself)
1½ minutes

THE EXOTIC BODY (2012)
Director: **Baz Luhrmann**
Additional Dialogue: **Baz Luhrmann**, Andrew Bolton, Schuyler
Weiss, and Sam Bromell (adapted from the writings of Elsa Schiaparelli)
Production and Costume Design: Catherine Martin
Producers: Anton Monsted and Schuyler Weiss
Cinematography: Josh Rothstein and Evan Papageorgiou
Editing: Jeremy Kotin
Cast: Judy Davis (as Elsa Schiaparelli) and Miuccia Prada (as herself)
2 minutes

NAIF CHIC (2012)
Director: **Baz Luhrmann**
Additional Dialogue: **Baz Luhrmann**, Andrew Bolton, Schuyler
Weiss, and Sam Bromell (adapted from the writings of Elsa Schiaparelli)
Production and Costume Design: Catherine Martin
Producers: Anton Monsted and Schuyler Weiss
Cinematography: Josh Rothstein and Evan Papageorgiou
Editing: Jeremy Kotin
Cast: Judy Davis (as Elsa Schiaparelli) and Miuccia Prada (as herself)
2 minutes

THE CLASSICAL BODY (2012)
Director: **Baz Luhrmann**
Additional Dialogue: **Baz Luhrmann**, Andrew Bolton, Schuyler
Weiss, and Sam Bromell (adapted from the writings of Elsa Schiaparelli)
Production and Costume Design: Catherine Martin
Producers: Anton Monsted and Schuyler Weiss
Cinematography: Josh Rothstein and Evan Papageorgiou
Editing: Jeremy Kotin
Cast: Judy Davis (as Elsa Schiaparelli) and Miuccia Prada (as herself)
1½ minutes

UGLY CHIC (2012)
Director: **Baz Luhrmann**
Additional Dialogue: **Baz Luhrmann**, Andrew Bolton, Schuyler
Weiss, and Sam Bromell (adapted from the writings of Elsa Schiaparelli)
Production and Costume Design: Catherine Martin
Producers: Anton Monsted and Schuyler Weiss
Cinematography: Josh Rothstein and Evan Papageorgiou

Editing: Jeremy Kotin
Cast: Judy Davis (as Elsa Schiaparelli) and Miuccia Prada (as herself)
1½ minutes

ELSA SCHIAPARELLI AND MIUCCIA PRADA: THE SURREAL BODY
(2012)
Director: **Baz Luhrmann**
Additional Dialogue: **Baz Luhrmann**, Andrew Bolton, Schuyler
Weiss, and Sam Bromell (adapted from the writings of Elsa Schiaparelli)
Production and Costume Design: Catherine Martin
Producers: Anton Monsted and Schuyler Weiss
Cinematography: Josh Rothstein and Evan Papageorgiou
Editing: Jeremy Kotin
Cast: Judy Davis (as Elsa Schiaparelli) and Miuccia Prada (as herself)
2½ minutes

As Actor

A COUNTRY PRACTICE (1981–1982)
 Luhrmann plays Jerry Percival in six episodes of the long-running TV
show (1981–1993).

WINTER OF OUR DREAMS (1981)
Written and directed by John Duigan. Starring Judy Davis and Bryan
Brown. Luhrmann plays Pete.

THE DARK ROOM (1982)
Co-written and directed by Paul Harmon. Starring Alan Cassell and
Anna Maria Monticelli. Luhrmann plays "First Student."

THE HIGHEST HONOR (1983)
Directed by Peter Maxwell and Seiji Maruyama. Starring Alan Cassell
and Steve Bisley. Luhrmann plays Able Seaman A. W. Huston.

KIDS OF THE CROSS (1983)
Shot and directed by Steve Mason (with Luhrmann as co-director). Part-
documentary in which Luhrmann plays a street kid in Sydney's Kings
Cross area.

Baz Luhrmann: Interviews

Stepping Out: Behind the Scenes of *Strictly Ballroom*

Ruth Hessey / 1992

From *Rolling Stone* (Australia), no. 474 (September 1992): 72–75, 92. Reprinted by permission of the author.

The South of France. Cannes. The 45th Festival International du Film. Cameras click. Poodles proliferate. And so do bleached blondes. There are almost more pet parlours in this town than bars. Outside the wedding-cake hotels which overlook the beach front (and the tonnes of imported white sand), tireless, jostling crowds wait for a glimpse of a movie star. Any movie star. Anything that moves.

Up on a dazzling balcony, Spike Lee is bagging white racists and handing out T-shirts for *Malcolm X*, his next film. Robert De Niro is invited to everything, and never turns up. Gerard Depardieu is trapped in his hotel room by the autograph hungry mobs. Vanessa Redgrave, Emma Thompson, Michael Douglas, Tom Selleck, John "Barton Fink" Turturro, even Sylvia Kristel, are all in town.

And down on one of the piers studded with media-soaked celebrities, a young Australian director is running through his festival success-story spiel. *The Player*, *Basic Instinct*, and *Howard's End* have had their go. As of day four of the festival, Baz Luhrmann's first feature film, *Strictly Ballroom*, is "the film" everyone is talking about in the bars and cafes (where it counts in Cannes). Already one overseas buyer has slept on the distributor's door, desperate to clinch a deal. At the first midnight screening, Festival audiences clapped and cheered during the film.

So Baz. Everyone loves you now.

Sipping Evian through a straw, suaver, craggier, and more visibly cranked up than you imagined possible on a deck chair, he squints into the blinding sun. "Well we didn't expect a ten-minute standing ovation," he admits. "I actually didn't know whether the Europeans would understand it." But they did.

"Hang on a sec," he says suddenly, grabbing his Instamatic. Whoopi Goldberg is being interviewed on the deck chair next door. "I love Whoopi," he apologizes, grabbing a holiday snap.

Not since *Crocodile Dundee* has an Australian film infatuated the market place to the *Strictly Ballroom* degree. Even the success of last year's surprise Australian hit, *Proof*, didn't translate into sales. By the end of the week, the film has sold to every major film distributor in the world.

"I've always had a little dream in the back of my head," says Luhrmann, adjusting a beach umbrella over his head, "that *Strictly Ballroom* would be one of the first audience-involving films, like *The Rocky Horror Show*. Films are always about the private experience. You don't yell out to the screen. But cinema is hungry again. I think the audience-involvement film could be where it's at. People want to cheer and clap."

People have been moved to clap, cheer, and stomp their feet during screenings of *Strictly Ballroom* all over the world: in Melbourne, in Paris and London, as well as Cannes.

Not bad for a low-budget, art-house film about ballroom dancing. Not bad for a first time director who grew up thinking he was a dag.

Baz, in a suit, is doing well in Cannes. His dance card is full. He's one of the few people—say five hundred—in town who will actually shake Robert De Niro's hand. Hollywood agents, always on the lookout for "the next Peter Weir" have him solidly booked for lunch. Robert Altman wants to chat. Back in Australia, his agency is already fielding calls from Steven Spielberg's office. Everyone connected with the *Strictly Ballroom* entourage has become the most handsome, witty, desirable person in town.

And every day Luhrmann is down here on celebrity pier with the team that made it happen. Long-standing, ever-ebullient cohorts, Catherine Martin and Bill Marron, the designers who've helped conceptualize not just *Strictly Ballroom* but every hit project Baz has done (opera, theatre, and film). Editor Jill Bilcock, who often worked forty-eight hours straight to get the final cut. Choreographer John O'Connell, co-writer Craig Pearce, Paul Mercurio, dancer and *Strictly Ballroom*'s sexy young star. They hover good-naturedly on the edge of every interview. They line up happily to take their bow after every major screening. They continue to work, feverishly, while Luhrmann fries in the media glare. Even when they're all exhausted the *Strictly Ballroom* show goes on. And, in this town of De Niros and Redgraves, it's the director of *Strictly Ballroom* who is the star.

"I'd never seen anyone so well prepared, and so committed to a project as Baz was," recalls Richard Payten, publicity director for Ronin Films, the small Australian distributor which gave *Strictly Ballroom* the guarantee it needed to qualify for funding from the Australian Film Commission (AFC).

"None of the majors wanted to get involved, and I think we were his last stop. But we took the risk. And I have to say it was Baz who convinced us. I realized that, if he could get half of his energy up on the screen, we'd have a fantastic film." Payten observed that, unlike some visionary autocrats, Luhrmann took time out to inspire everyone. "He gave the same amount of energy to the publicity assistant as he gave to the cinematographer. He made everyone want to give 110 percent."

With that sort of excitement on set, even before it was finished, the vibe on *Strictly Ballroom* was good. "We had a film we were proud of, even if it bombed," recalls Catherine Martin.

However, making it a financial success wasn't such a sure thing. Ronin and overseas distributors Beyond International knew that they had an uphill battle on their hands. It was obvious the film had several major disadvantages in commercial terms. No stars, no precedent, no hook. What was it about exactly? Something about dancing your own steps and a life half lived in fear? The *Strictly Ballroom* team arrived in Cannes with a modest objective, and proceeded to leaflet every pigeon-hole in town "to get the interest up."

By the end of the festival, it was quite a different story. "You had to be there to understand the magnitude of the response," recalls John Thornhill, publicity director at Beyond. "After the first day, we threw the appointment book away. They were crawling over dead bodies to get to us. We were offered bribes. We were offered post-dated cheques. We were offered deals by people before they'd even seen the film."

"In ten years I've never seen anything like it," agrees Pressanna Vasudevan, development manager with the London office of the AFC. "It was *Saturday Night Fever* meets Almodovar. The AFC helped finance the film. Then it just leapt out of our hands."

And it wasn't just the Americans who were going bananas over *Strictly Ballroom*. The French loved it even before it arrived in Cannes. Ronin had been prepping the Japanese arthouse market for a year, and, after the Cannes screenings, *Strictly Ballroom* was snapped up by distributors throughout Europe and even in Korea.

All this from a $A3.5 million movie with a title no-one could pronounce, lashings of Aussie kitsch, screechingly broad accents, not one "name" actor in the cast, and a plot so simple it was almost twee.

Obviously, *Strictly Ballroom* was not tailored to some sort of homogeneous formula for overseas success.

"It was practically a contractual obligation that I levelled at everyone, that we weren't going to mimic American or European film," says Luhrmann. "If Hollywood had made it, *Strictly Ballroom* would have been totally earnest. It would have been *Dirty Dancing*."

Luhrmann didn't want to make a naturalistic film. If anything, his goal was to recapture something of the kitsch surreality of his Australian childhood. "In Australia we're embarrassed by our own culture. But we are fresh, we are original because we are not in the American-Euro scene."

So he went ahead and made a low-budget pic about being embarrassed which turned out to be perfect pop.

"Well, fuck it. I was ballroom dancing when I was a kid. That's our culture, call it kitsch if you like. But we can celebrate that; it's as relevant as anything else. Marilyn Monroe and James Dean were considered the pulpiest, kitschiest of Kylie Minogues in their time. Years later they're cultural icons." He glances across the Mediterranean as a string of reporters line up for their slot. "Time makes art," he says.

Time and determination. Like the hero of *Strictly Ballroom*, a dancer who has to fight the "all powerful federation" to dance his own steps his own way, Luhrmann had to fight to make *Strictly Ballroom* the way he knew it should be made. There is still a cupboard at the *Strictly Ballroom* production office stuffed with rejected drafts of the film. "I kid you not!" Luhrmann yodels. "To this day there's a script with a car chase in it. The producers went to the Americans, and the Film Finance Corporation (FFC) were saying it's gotta be this, it's got to be that. I was powerless to convince people unless we showed them. Thank God we pulled it back to the idea we originally had."

What he originally had was a play. A thirty-minute, NIDA-student-devised theatre piece based on an idea Luhrmann talked the others into with a puff of tulle and the words "Cha Cha." (Even then he was good at pitching a deal.) Luhrmann took the production to a student festival in Czechoslovakia and won an award for best direction there.

After graduation, the original cast dispersed, but the idea of *Strictly Ballroom* did not. Having the foresight to buy out the other contributors' rights to the idea, Luhrmann took another crack at it during a year-long stint as artistic director for a fledgling company of Sydney's brightest for the Sydney Theatre Company. He remounted a new seventy-minute version enlarged by the contributions of a new cast.

"By the time we made it a ninety-minute screenplay, a whole different leap was made," he says. "The huge battles were all about convincing people of the ideas. In Australia we're so willing to put money into other areas, but the person with the type-writer, can't they do it in six weeks?

"The struggle of Scott was nothing compared to the 'all powerful federation' I was fighting in the FFC. If I hadn't already done it as a play, and if I hadn't had the support of producers who financed us to keep going with the screenplay until we got what we wanted, the whole thing would never have worked."

The process was exhausting, but Luhrmann was honing his storytelling skills, and herein lies the secret of his adroit cinematic debut.

"Storytelling is about telling and telling and telling it," he explains. "That's how you make a great story. When I was trying to get the show on the road, in the very early days, I had to tell the story of *Strictly Ballroom* maybe five times a day, to the greatest variety of people. And the more you test an idea, the stronger it is."

Several months later, *Strictly Ballroom* fever has hit Sydney. And it's somehow fitting that, having been thoroughly licked over by what he calls the "schmooze machine," Luhrmann recalls the low points of his life while taking a break from publicity on a traffic island in the middle of Sydney's Taylor Square.

The aptly named Gilligan's Island (a cheap paradise for drunks overlooked by the inner-city's zooshier bars) hunches its scuffed cheeks at the foot of a ragged bunch of imported palms. The foreshore is papered with rock posters. A handsome derelict who looks eerily like Val Kilmer stares malevolently at the besuited Luhrmann, who's been slicked up and gloated over by a bevy of makeup artists from *Premiere* magazine for the past four hours. This was the only place to get away.

"It's all a bit too busy and silly at the moment," Luhrmann says. His tan facial-pancake marks a cartoonlike daub of success against the dusty intersection. He's just heard about the audience response at a critics' screening in London. You guessed it. They clapped and cheered. And the *London Times* enthuses that he's "reinvented romantic burlesque."

Even if *Strictly Ballroom* flops in Australia, it's made its money back. Luhrmann is just starting to articulate "the magic of this film," when the handsome derelict gets to his feet, swaying under a dying palm. "Fuck you," he spits in disgust, and staggers off the island towards the traffic lights of some lost Broadway.

"I get that a lot," Luhrmann says, rather dryly. "From quite sane people. This is not a great country for success." Certainly he's a long way from Cannes and the company of Spike Lee and Hal Hartley: "They've gone way beyond local politics," he says. "Politics is a euphemism for bitchiness. All they care about is making something really well."

Here in Australia, Luhrmann smells the odd whiff of sour grapes. "If you demonstrate an absolutely pathological determination to achieve something, a lot of people hate you for it round here. It's an Aussie disease."

Yes, Luhrmann has been called an arrogant prick in his time.

"When you take people on a journey and it's a success, everyone loves you," he points out. "If you take them and the ship sinks, the hatred and anger is so intense, it's almost unbearable."

About five years ago, the Six Years Old Company was Luhrmann's first professional gig as a theatre company director. Instigated by the Sydney Theatre Company to encourage young blood, it was a project with no lack of brilliantine in the wings. But the year-long program, even with an earlier incarnation of *Strictly Ballroom* on board, was almost universally panned. "That was as low as I ever want to go."

But now, from the heights of Gilligan's Island, he waxes philosophical.

"If you look at any sustained artistic success, it's about long-term creative relationships," he explains. "At Six Years Old, we had all the bright young people in one room, but they had nothing to do with what I wanted to achieve. In fact, at times, they were diametrically opposed to it."

Basically, Luhrmann hadn't yet refined his team. He was still looking for the place he belonged, and the people who would surround him. Ironically, the attention he got is, he says, what turned him around. "I decided from that moment on to listen to my instincts, and to work from them."

Since then his career path has been relatively straightforward. "I've just made plans, and stuck to them. People ask me why I swap mediums so much. It's because I think, wouldn't it be great to bring an Italian opera to our contemporaries, and wouldn't it be great to go and live in France and research it, and hang out where it was written in Italy?"

"It sounds corny, but you follow a map, and then you get lost and you make another map, until you get there. I don't know whether I'm more exceptional at trying to get somewhere than anyone else."

Maps, journeys, casualties, side-swipes. These are all part of the *Strictly Ballroom* Baz monologue, and not-so-strange coming from someone who grew up on the road, literally a "service station/pig farm in the middle of nowhere," Herons Creek, NSW.

Luhrmann senior is an ex-Navy commander turned gardener. One brother has an orange juice factory, the other is a policeman. "I had a joyous childhood, but it was extremely tumultuous as well," says Luhrmann. "Do you remember what it meant to have even mildly short hair in the seventies? We had crew cuts.

"Living on a service station, we saw everyone from the Bee Gees to the Hells Angels to gypsies come by. It was an endless cavalcade of characters, and car accidents. Our lives were full of blood and death. It was very dramatic." It certainly wasn't the high camp fantasia of ballroom dancing. Luhrmann eventually made good his escape, to Sydney, and showbiz.

"I ran away as a kid. My parents broke up, and my mother left our family, and—to cut a long story short—at a certain point in my life, I ran away, and I found her in the city. I was sixteen or seventeen, in my last year of high school."

Once he got to Sydney, Luhrmann says he spent the next few years trying to act cool. "I didn't want to be a dag from the country, but I felt like such a boring, insignificant person. I thought I was lucky to get my first acting job. I was extremely self-conscious."

Virtually since that time, he has enlisted the creative skills of dozens of others to make that story into a film. While he pursued a career as an actor, as a theatre director, and in opera, where he created the smash hit production of *La Boheme* for the Australian Opera (which is having a second run later this year), Luhrmann was still working on the idea of *Strictly Ballroom*. He was in the process of making his own experience into a universal theme.

"It's like being a bit of a dag at school, and you're so desperate to be accepted by everyone else, you can't be yourself," he says, "and that's the story of Fran (the ugly duckling dancer in the film). Fran isn't about an ugly girl who becomes beautiful. Fran is about all of us when we all feel stupid, about what we're all too scared to be."

There's more than a skerrick of Fran in Luhrmann. Luhrmann isn't the star of *Strictly Ballroom* because he hogs the limelight, or because he did it all on his own. On the contrary, it's simply that the awkward angry pushy kid with the crew cut realized who he could be.

"Once you work with people, you realize, no matter how clever they are, they're all scared. I like actors and I really feel for them. And they're just absolutely fucking scared, because all the attention is on them."

Understanding this, Luhrmann managed to push his film right to the edge, encouraging in some of the characters a monster-like tinge. "As long as you park in your naturalistic performance, people think you're a genius in film. But I know people who are more extreme than that. Life is much more extreme than that. It's much more like opera. Films usually water it down."

Luhrmann stands up, the rush of words momentarily spent. For a brief moment he towers over Gilligan's Island. "They say I'm good for three turkeys," he grins, brushing the island detritus from his pants. "And that's great, you know. Everything's great. The media attention's great. Big American picture offers are great. I've got much more power now to do what I want, and that's great. But ultimately nothing's changed. I've still got to come up with ideas that I really love and know would be fun to do." Back at headquarters, Bill Marron and Catherine Martin are already working on one or two.

Ten years ago, Baz Luhrmann was just a dag from the middle of nowhere. So were most Australians. Something definitely has changed.

More than Romance Colors
Strictly Ballroom

Peter Brunette / 1993

First published in the *New York Times*, February 7, 1993. Reprinted by permission of the author's estate.

Festival audiences are notoriously undemanding, but a standing ovation? That's what greeted *Strictly Ballroom*, by the first-time filmmaker, Baz Luhrmann, when it was screened last fall at the Toronto Film Festival. So it's not the audience that worries the Australian director as he anticipates the film's opening in New York on Friday; it's the critics. "Everywhere we go, there are critics who are absolutely, pathologically in love with the film," he says, "and then there are others who don't just dismiss it, they absolutely hate it, because it offends those things that they've come to believe define good filmmaking. It doesn't have indicative symbols that this is art."

Janet Maslin, reviewing the film in the *New York Times* during the New York Film Festival last fall, called it "pure corn," adding, "but it's corn that has been overlaid with a buoyant veneer of spangles and marabou, and with a tireless sense of fun."

Mr. Luhrmann unashamedly calls *Strictly Ballroom* a "myth" or "fairytale." The film tells the story of a young man (played by Paul Mercurio) who, in his quest for the Pan-Pacific dance trophy, dares to break the rules of the "all-powerful" Ballroom Dancing Federation by inventing new steps. Along the way, he rescues Fran (Tara Morice), an ugly-duckling child of Spanish immigrants, from her shyness and awkwardness. And she in turn helps him win the championship. Of course, they fall in love.

According to Mr. Luhrmann, who is thirty, the audience is supposed to know from the beginning how the film will end. "Once that contract is made in the first fifteen minutes, you know that I'm saying to you that this is a fairy tale, and you either accept that contract or you don't. Every character in the film is a stereotype. It's like in Moliere: you absolutely know who Mr. Sycophant is the moment he walks in the door. But stereotypes are only offensive when they're placed within a set of naturalistic conventions and pretend to be reality."

Many reviewers have likened the film to *Rocky*, but Mr. Luhrmann isn't happy with the comparison. "The myth in *Rocky* and my myth are the same myth," he admits. "But there's a big, big difference, because *Rocky* tries to convey this myth as reality. I don't. Take a more extreme example, a film I really like, *Taxi Driver*. This is the damsel-in-the-tower myth, but it's made so gritty and real, like a documentary, that people are thinking, 'This is the mark of great film: look how real it is.' In our film, we try to disarm you by walking that fine line of sending it up and then twisting it so that you also have an emotional response."

Wendy Keys, executive producer for programming at the Film Society of Lincoln Center and a member of the selection committee for the New York Film Festival, said *Strictly Ballroom* was chosen for the festival "because it was life-affirming, joyous, and humanitarian. It's full of optimism and willing to take a chance on being sentimental. It's nice to see filmmakers trying to be something besides nasty and dark."

In casting the principal roles, Mr. Luhrmann stuck religiously to his conviction that, in contrast to most dance films, acting had to be paramount. "The acting ability is more important than the dancing, because you can act dancing but not dance acting."

This emphasis comes from Mr. Luhrmann's background in directing opera and theater; in fact, *Strictly Ballroom* originated as a play. The inspiration for the story, curiously, was the Cold War. Mr. Luhrmann and a small group of actors were working together in 1985, and they would discuss the fact that they weren't as active in demonstrating for peace as young people in the sixties and seventies. Yet they still felt enormous anxiety about the possibility of nuclear war. Mr. Luhrmann wanted to explore that concern in his work, but decided against a standard dramatic approach. Because he had been involved in ballroom dancing as a teenager (when his parents separated, his father thought it might help keep the rest of the family together), it seemed natural to look there. Mr. Luhrmann also discovered that his mother, who had disappeared after the separation, had, by coincidence, become a ballroom-dancing instructor.

"I realized that it was a fantastic microcosm of the world at large," Mr. Luhrmann says. "They were the same kind of desperate political power-mongers. We toured the play version in Czechoslovakia at the time Communism was still very much around, and the Czechs would climb up on the stage going 'Bravo!' For them, the all-powerful Federation had nothing to do with ballroom dancing. To me, the film is not about ballroom dancing. It's about overcoming oppression, whatever nature that oppression takes."

Mr. Luhrmann's earliest acting and directing experiences were heavily weighted toward psychological realism, which he now disdains. At age eighteen, he left his hometown, a six-house speck on the map, and ran away to Sydney, where he lived with a gang for a while. There, he participated in a television documentary on street life. "I learned that documentary is never, ever true. It's always a manipulation of reality as soon as you choose ninety minutes out of a life and put music under it." He feels that drama is more honest because the audience knows it's only a story, told from a specific point of view.

The best drama, he believes, was produced by artists who were fully engaged in the popular culture of their day, like Puccini (whose work he calls "the soap opera of his time") and Mozart, whose *Magic Flute* he likens in entertainment value to the Universal Studio tour. His current model is Shakespeare, whose wide appeal he feels "driven" to emulate. Future projects include the staging of Benjamin Britten's opera *A Midsummer Night's Dream*, and perhaps a rock opera for a producer in Paris.

Mr. Luhrmann does not see himself as an auteur, but rather as "part of a team that makes things." That team consists of Catherine Martin, the film's production designer, and Bill Marron, the associate production designer, both of whom share a house with Mr. Luhrmann in Sydney. At the moment, they are building a house together and hope a film will come out of that experience.

In any case, he is firmly committed to a populist approach to the arts. "I turned against my family when I first began creating," he says. "I wanted to make things that they could not understand, that said, 'You are dumb. I am clever.' I wanted to say, 'Look, I'm working on Strindberg here.' And now I think I've grown through that. I really want my mother to have a response to something that my cynical, complex, major intellectual friends also get a reading from. Honestly, it would be a much easier thing for me to have made a grainy, socially real flick. I know that the moment you stick a happy ending on it you're going to get panned. But Shakespeare had no problem with it."

Romeo + Juliet: "Appear Thou in the Likeness of a Sigh . . ."

Mark Mordue / 1997

From *Australian Style*, January 1997. Reprinted by permission of the author.

When I catch up with Baz Luhrmann, the Australian director whose *Romeo + Juliet* is number one at the American box office, he has "flown the coop" and is on a road trip across America. "I've got away from the circus we've been doing," he says of the media blitz. His version of *Romeo and Juliet* is also a circus in its own right, ultra-modern, splashy, and stylish, melding Latino street cool, pop-culture speed, and Elizabethan stage language with the theatrical dash of *Natural Born Killers*. After Luhrmann's first film, *Strictly Ballroom*, his new one is a quantum leap, with shining performances from its leads, Leonardo DiCaprio and Claire Danes. Talking to the filmmaker, one can sense a compacted confidence that spills into the way he emphatically accents words. You can almost feel American success massed underneath and contained. Luhrmann spoke to me from the heart of the Nevada Desert: "My team and I usually spend our time in LA or New York, or Miami, where we wrote *Romeo + Juliet*. But to understand America, you've really got to go into the middle."

Mark Mordue: It's funny that you're in the desert. There was a vicious westerly in Sydney a day ago. It was so dry and bitter, so intense, I didn't know whether to break down and cry or kill someone.
Baz Luhrmann: Really? Oh yeah, I remember those in Sydney. Spooky.

MM: I've always liked that in Shakespeare's plays—the idea of a cosmos out of kilter—and the way it relates to the souls of the antagonists and their world. Was that important to you?
BL: It was an absolute, given that people then believed natural signs and symbols were indicative of the way in which the world was going. So

14

there's a very specific reason why there's a discussion in the film about this kind of wind you talk of, that "blows us from our course." Every decision made in the film came out of a long and meticulous analysis of the Elizabethan world.

MM: I love the way you've adapted *Romeo + Juliet* to the present by brewing up a pop culture storm with it.

BL: I'll tell you something about pop culture in terms of this film. At the moment, there's a storm in the US about it—people are running round saying, "How come William Shakespeare is number one at the box office?" And others are going, "How come the style changes every thirty-five seconds?" The easy answer is that, as everyone says, it's an MTV version. But in fact we drew our style, if you like "the pop style," from *the* pop king—and the King of Pop in the Elizabethan world was William Shakespeare.

I mean, you'd die faced with three thousand drunken screaming punters. You would do anything, but anything, to grab their attention and pull them into focus and tell your story. So, with Shakespeare, you have one moment of stand-up comedy, followed by a popular song, followed by incredible violence, followed by pure drama. All those elements are written into the text, or already existed in the Elizabethan productions of *Romeo + Juliet*.

MM: I found the energy inspiring, although a part of me felt an odd kind of sadness. I guess, in this weird way, because I'm thirty-six, I felt a strange sense of divorce from that passion. Even, if I'm honest, almost a bit of jealousy about it.

BL: That's interesting, Mark. And I think it's exactly what the piece is about. I mean, lots of young people rush out to see it and go, "Hey I get the idea of love as an out of control sports car, as a drug." But we people who have passed through that—once you've had that first hit and it doesn't kill you, as it does Romeo and Juliet—once you survive that, you control it. You learn to drive your car. But the memory remains.

So the really big idea in the piece is about what it means for the adult world. Which is: don't go passing your prejudice, or your judgment, or your bitterness, or your anger, down to younger people. Because in a world of learned hate, innocents are going to get killed and you're going to lose something you love. So the point is that you sit there as an older person and go, "Yeah, I remember what that was like. I remember how it was to be out of control with love."

MM: Lately a new cinema language seems to be evolving. Oliver Stone's *Natural Born Killers* is obviously a part of that. I wondered how it influenced you. And I also wonder how you see cinema language shifting generally and what you make of those who dismiss things as "MTV." It's as if people are living in an old narrative space and don't know how to cope with this new language.

BL: Look, I agree with all those points. It's a huge subject. I remember being at an early screening of *Natural Born Killers* with Oliver Stone, before he did the final cut, and he actually *was* mimicking MTV. But I think the choices *we made* for *Romeo + Juliet* came from the understanding that Shakespeare would do anything to engage audiences and tell a story. Having said that, the reason our audience *can* make sense of how we're telling them the story has something to do with MTV. And with television news and commercials.

I wasn't influenced by *Natural Born Killers*. . . . Maybe I was . . . I don't know. But I'll tell you, I have been influenced by the style of Hindi movies. If you look at an Indian movie, a really great Indian movie: it goes for three hours, and it has a Busby Berkeley musical routine, and then it will have the most violent murder scene next to it. . . .

It makes complete sense for us to do that too. You think of Victorian eclecticism. Because what we are doing is: *we are summing up.* We are moving towards the end of a millennium. We're at the end of a big period. And we're summing up everything that has come before.

MM: As soon as I saw *Romeo + Juliet*, I thought, "Wow, teenagers are going to see this and go oooff!"

BL: Well that has certainly happened. I'm trying to avoid saying this, but in fact it's true: younger people just get it. And if there's a fight in America over it being good or bad for Shakespeare, Europeans and Australians just go "yeah!" Because people outside of America look at the world as . . . Australians *particularly* look at the world as being made up of bits, and have no problem with a Europeanness mixed with an Americanness that ultimately, I hope, makes up a third element.

MM: What about your style of filmmaking, which has a very camp and flamboyant edge? I wondered how much gay culture's been an influence on you?

BL: Well, I think the whole of Australia is a bit gay. . . . Camp is a style that's been around for a long, long time. To quote Oscar Wilde, it's dealing with a very serious subject matter in a very silly way, so that you *can* deal with it. It's really just a style of wit. The world has been bogged down by an over-cerebral perspective on things. I think to disarm those who take a basic cold, intellectual approach to everything is a great strategy. That's not to say that what we're doing has no meaning. Everything we do is strong, everything we do is decorative, and everything we do is our style. You can say it is camp or gay or whatever—what that means, in truth, is that it's disarmingly fun, but it deals with something of meaning. Certainly of meaning to us.

MM: In the wake of *Strictly Ballroom* and *Muriel's Wedding* and *Priscilla*, a certain kitsch stylisation is now embedded in Australian cinema, something a little too stereotypical. Have you been held to account for that?
BL: A little bit. But the choice is this: I could have been a very, very rich man today by accepting the many, many offers for millions of dollars to simply fit into the system and say, "Oh yeah, we'll do that American movie with that American script."

But we didn't. And I must say "we": *Romeo + Juliet* is an Australian-Canadian co-production, but it is an Australian film. We "pre" and "posted" it in Australia and it was shot with an Australian team. We worked with Fellini's hair and make-up people—different people who we thought were brilliant from around the world—but *we made our thing*. We decided to make it. We went out and made it. And we made it in *our style*.

The European press refer to it as "Fellini-esque." They don't say it's "Australian kitsch stylization," not that I *mind* if people say that. It's our style. *It's the way we tell*. You think we're going to relinquish that? For what? To embrace what some pretentious person decides is art? What is less artful about what Fellini does or what Oscar Wilde does? Does *it* have less meaning!?

I don't mind being held to account for opening a door to do that. I don't say it's the only style, but it *is* the way we see things. One of the things I learnt from David Hockney—whom I got to know because he's a great fan of my operas—is that he makes a decision about the *way* he sees things. He says, "Whatever you do, don't *judge* the way you see it." I've seen many, many Australian pure creatives become self-conscious about their style because a whole bunch of people have said, "Uh oh!" Big deal. In truth, style is truth to us. That's all that really matters.

MM: You have a thing about reacting to institutionalization. . . .
BL: Yes, I do.

MM: It was a prevalent theme in both *Strictly Ballroom* and *Romeo + Juliet*. Can you comment on where it comes from?

BL: There is something linking both the films. I don't want to get too self-conscious about it, but let me say that, clearly, the trick with *Strictly Ballroom* was to create something very simple that, like Shakespeare, could be read both as a simple story, as light entertainment, and in terms of its bigger ideas. And the bigger idea of *Strictly Ballroom* is about artistic repression.

With *Romeo + Juliet*, we actually took about a year to convince the studios that we should do it in this manner. And while it might be about the adult world telling these young lovers that they can't love this person because of their names, it could easily be because of their race, their sexuality, or their religion.

I get angry about this, about the way that institutions are constantly at odds with creative endeavours. We were told when we were trying to make *Strictly Ballroom*, "Oh, Australian films aren't like that. It'll never work; no one will want to see that." We had to fight.

And I am passionate about this subject because I think that one of the distinctive things about Australians is that we allow ourselves to be repressed because a lot of fear-loaded people say, "Uh, that makes me uncomfortable." I remember once driving in Sydney with a taxi driver. It was in 1988, the year of the bicentenary, and there was discussion about how we should spend the money to celebrate the occasion. He said, "I reckon they should build a museum to all the truly great, great ideas that Australians have had, that they've had to go overseas and make, and that have been sold back to Australia." That really stuck with me. I thought, "You're right, you know. The beginnings of the computer. The beginnings of television. . . ."

It's changed now, and that's why I'm coming back to Australia to make films from there. Imagination is so *potent* in Australia, but the struggle continues. We have to believe in our own imagination, because—let's face it—in a world where technology takes care of the rest, imagination is the only valuable asset. I don't think I'm the only person to say that. I think Einstein had a little phrase that wasn't too dissimilar. It's true. What is going to become more and more valuable as time goes on? Only imagination.

MM: Which is an instinct or a map?
BL: It is an instinct. Hollywood is a place full of scared people. And people who do what we do are paid to have an instinct. It's not that we know. It's not that anybody knows. It's that you have a strong instinct. And people come to say, "Hmm, that Baz Luhrmann and his team, they seem

to have a strong instinct about what to tell and what to do." That's really all it is.

MM: Can you tell me about Leonardo DiCaprio? You've said you feel that he "defines a generation."

BL: I have never anything but great things to say about D. Think of this: at the same time that we were trying to get this film made, he was being offered the incomes of small nations to make other movies. I mean three to four million dollars for a picture. But, for no money, he came to Australia, flying coach, and put himself up with his father twice to work with me to get *Romeo + Juliet* made. And that is something to do with his generation. Because, unlike the eighties Brat Pack, here is an extraordinarily talented young actor who is saying, "Hmm! In the end a lot of money is only a lot of money. How many hotels can you stay in? How big a pool can you have?" What he really cares about is fine acting. That's what I love about D. He is just in love with the art of acting.

MM: That's interesting because, when I look at him, I wonder whether he is primed for fucked-upness, and whether he is another River Phoenix on the burn?

BL: He is an incredibly down-to-earth guy, just absolutely adorable as a human being, fantastically bright, and just remarkably talented. When you have all of those things and are the focus of such adoration, it is a hard, hard thing not to be consumed by it.

If anyone has a chance of surviving it and growing, Leonardo does. It's very easy for those of us who don't have to deal with it to say, "Oh, what's he got to complain about? He's a movie star." But I know, because I see D. a lot—he's currently doing this big *Titanic* film with James Cameron and is having to deal with the explosion of this film, at number one, doing Shakespeare—he's gone from being "that interesting young actor" to the Beatles. People can say what they like, but that's not an easy thing to do.

MM: I love that line: "Appear thou in the likeness of a sigh." One of the qualities that struck me about Leonardo is he manages to do that. There's quite a feminine quality to him. I was wondering if you were aware of making that feminine quality heroic in the film.

BL: Oooh, yeah. The thing about it—why is he such great representation of a generation?—is that he's neither man nor woman and neither boy nor man. He doesn't have these pumping muscles. He's a sort of

anti-hero. We based the character of Romeo on James Dean and Kurt Cobain. I mean, he comes on the screen and girls scream, but at the same
time he's this very wispy looking character. So you have to say, "What
is it they're connecting with?" And I think they're connecting with the
fact he is androgynous and is, as a person, so comfortable in himself. I'm
not sure the rest of the world is all that comfortable with him, and I hope
that that doesn't become a problem.

MM: How about Claire Danes? I noticed her first in *Little Women* and
even though she was only on the screen for a short time, she radiated
this luminous, calm quality. It was so pure.
BL: Well, Mark, I looked all around the world for Juliet. I saw maybe sixty
Juliets, some of the most famous and finest young actors. I knew I had to
find someone who was strong and grounded. And ultimately it was the
same with Claire as it was with Leonardo—it was like a flash of lightning.
She was the only actress who came up to Leonardo and kissed him on the
lips, and Leonardo actually took notice. D. always says she was the one
that really made him go "Whuuur!" The strength of her against Leonardo was a key requisite. But she is sixteen. And that's the difference.

Pete Postlethwaite was playing Father Laurence, and he was saying for
a while, "Oh, Bazza, the age-old problem of finding a sixteen year old
who can act like a thirty year old. Good Luck!" And it was very difficult.
It was only because Jane Campion said, "Have you seen Claire Danes?"
She was casting *Portrait of a Lady* at the time, and she said, "You should
check out Claire Bear," as she calls her. And I did. Then I had someone
who could handle Leonardo and not be blown off the screen by him, and
that's no easy task.

MM: Yeah. She just struck me so strongly. This sounds over the top, but
it was almost like seeing a saint.
BL: Well, I'll tell you what. When I was a kid I worked with Judy Davis.
And she has that quality too: fragile but strong. Claire is really similar to
that. She brings you that unearthly quality.

MM: America is such a bizarre, copycat culture. It imitates so much. Did
dealing with the topic of suicide worry you? How to treat it? How you
might be accused of ennobling something like that?
BL: It was a huge issue for us, a huge issue. And a lot of the time there
was discussion with the studio about doing the suicide off-screen. But,
unless you change the end of the story, ultimately the story is about two

young people who commit suicide. And I wasn't about to do that. While we were making the film there was almost an identical teenage suicide in an identical setting in Miami. The fact that it happens all the time is the reason that the story exists.

I think the most dangerous thing would have been to treat it like a soap ad and not deal with it in a strong way, to have it pleasantly happen off-screen: and there they are, dead in a pretty manner. To deal with it as a confronting thing was really the only solution.

But it is an issue. We simply dealt with the story as honestly and as simply and as powerfully as we could. And then the ramifications of that . . . because it will happen: at some point the story will happen again, because it does. And then someone will say, "Oh, influenced by *Romeo + Juliet*." But whether or not that is the case you can never tell. You can only tell stories honestly.

Baz Luhrmann's *William Shakespeare's Romeo + Juliet*

Pauline Adamek / 1997

From *Cinema Papers*, no. 114 (February 1997). Reprinted by permission of the author.

20th Century Fox is buzzing with the news. *Romeo + Juliet* is number one at the box office during its opening weekend, taking $US11.1 million on 1,277 screens and beating its closest contender (one of those comedian-with-an-elephant buddy movies) by three times over.

Baz is excited. "I thought it would stir up an interest. But we were relentlessly told that youth are uninterested in Shakespeare and that they would not want to see *Romeo and Juliet*. Some critics have come out and said there are bad films, there are the worst films of all time, and then there's Baz Luhrmann's *Romeo + Juliet*. To them it is that bad and confronting and I understand that, but we told it in our way."

The "we" Luhrmann frequently refers to are his longtime collaborators, in particular production designer Catherine Martin and screenwriter Craig Pearce, with whom he studied at NIDA during the early eighties. The creative team has grown since the *Strictly Ballroom* days to include producer-art director Martin Brown, editor Jill Bilcock, and choreographer John "Cha-Cha" O'Connell. Hence, their company is now called BAZMARK Productions to incorporate the two Martins.

With this, his second film, Luhrmann has shot a highly stylized—at times frenetic—gangland version of the world's most enduring tragic and romantic fable. His intention was to reveal the power of Shakespeare's four-hundred-year-old myth, which is not so much about young love as about the belief that the inheritance of hatred, anger, and bitterness within a culture or family inexorably leads to tragedy.

To date, the film's audience has been made up of a high proportion of teenage girls and young women. Its success has proven that the two young leads, Leonardo DiCaprio and Claire Danes, have a strong enough following to open a film. Made for a sum of between $US15–17 million, clearly *Romeo + Juliet* will have no trouble making its money back and possibly a decent profit, as proven by a healthy $US9 million take for the second weekend.

Luhrmann maintains that this is the first time a major studio has taken the chance on a Shakespearean adaptation and that even independent productions such as Kenneth Branagh's *Much Ado About Nothing* only took $US20 million domestically. Although the Mexico City shoot was shut down due to illness, hurricanes, and a kidnapping, Luhrmann says the hardest part of the job was convincing the studio to give the go-ahead to the film.

"It was very difficult to convince people, to convince Fox. It's hard to believe that a studio made this film at the level at which it is financed, which is essentially experimental in its execution. People say Hollywood is in love with Shakespeare. That's not true. Why do you think majors don't bother? They're not worth the biscuits."

On the wings of the film's strong opening weekend, 20th Century Fox has signed Luhrmann to an exclusive, two-year deal that calls for him to write, direct, and produce for the studio. With an office on the studio's US lot and another in Sydney, Luhrmann will not start the developmental process for another two months. He has even turned down an invitation to stage an opera at London's Covent Garden. Several other studios were making offers but Luhrmann decided to stay with the one that had brought him to Hollywood. He felt that News Corporation president and CEO Peter Chernin and Fox Filmed Entertainment president and CEO Bill Mechanic had taken a big risk when they gave the go-ahead to *Romeo + Juliet*.

If it was a gamble, with an entire budget less than certain stars' salaries, then it certainly has paid off. Surely the finest cinematic experience you could ask for is the pure magic of watching fresh, young love unfurl before your eyes. In the scene when the lovers first meet, gazing through a gorgeous aquarium, actors Leonardo DiCaprio and Claire Danes personify love at first sight, their faces suffused with delight and sweetness. It's as if we are watching cinema history unfold, witnessing the emergence of a legendary screen duo for our time. If this were the 1940s, we could expect half a dozen more films starring this compatible pair.

How much of the success of the film is down to the casting? "There's no question that you have in Leonardo and Claire two fine young actors, remembering that when I cast Leonardo, two years ago, he was unknown. He had just been nominated for *What's Eating Gilbert Grape*.

Claire was just on television (in *My So-Called Life*). They absolutely have a following and are responsible for people being interested. But remember this: Leonardo has not opened a film on his own. He has not even done vague box office. Claire has never opened a film. So are they alone responsible for the box office? Obviously somewhat, and also they're good actors."

Why did you choose them, when they weren't that big? "Well, D. I just looked at and thought he looked liked Romeo. Sort of like James Dean, and Romeo was your first 'rebel without a cause,' your first Byronesque 'I'm rebelling but have no political cause to rebel against' character. So I rang him up and he and his father came down to Australia and spent their own money and flew economy. They came down twice and we shot a workshop on video and finally convinced the studio to let us do it. Claire: I searched the world; I saw actors all over the world. And then Jane Campion, who lives near me in Sydney, said, 'Have you seen Claire on *My So-Called Life?*' Which I hadn't, so I went back to the US and Claire came in. I was looking for someone who was sixteen but who had the strength of character to deal with Leonardo, because he is a formidable opponent in the acting stakes. Plus most of the young girls were like, [Baz mimes swooning and heart fluttering] 'My god, Leonardo!' so that's undermining, to work with someone you find attractive when you're sixteen. She just walked right up to him and said, 'Art thou not Romeo and a Montague?' and kissed him. They were strong. It is crucial, because the film is so frenetic, that, when they get together, you need time to stand still. I don't expect everyone to get it, but I think they do achieve that. I think they do bring a stillness to the film."

There is an unusual rhythm to the film: from the frenzied energy of the brawls and the Bacchanalian excesses of the ball to the serenity of the romantic scenes between the young couple. Dispensing with formula on all fronts, the film's use of Shakespeare's text feels rushed. It is yelled, mumbled, whispered, bawled, and burbled. No one, except possibly Pete Postlethwaite as an ornately tattooed Father Laurence, seems to know how to find the metre that underpins the poetry. Thus, what we lose, particularly in the first scene between the lovers, is the grace of the poetry that spontaneously falls from their lips. They match each other with witty epigrams and end up speaking in perfect sonnets.

That Luhrmann audaciously stages the balcony scene with Romeo and Juliet treading water is in keeping with his motif that these two escape into water. They use water for silence, for peace and, as Luhrmann puts it, for "their 'there's a place for us' moments." Luhrmann deals with their world as if their parents are in a Busby Berkeley musical on acid, all mania and relentless hysteria. "That final image when they kiss under water—it's just silence."

In a stroke of innovative genius, Luhrmann has used the device of television as the storyteller and shows the prologue and epilogue on a TV screen in the centre of our movie screen. The two key speeches are uttered by the newsreader with just the right combination of newspeak intonation and solemn poetry. To Luhrmann, television is the chorus of our lives.

While the poetic force is diminished, the brash presentation and sheer accessibility of one of the most treasured works of English literature more than makes up for the loss. Then there is the film's pace. Bilcock brings a tremendous energy to the film, with her rapid-fire editing and sculptural vision. Again, the television mentality is present as Luhrmann frequently pounds his thumb firmly on the fast-forward button. "I wanted to zip through the city and through any boring bits."

As always with the creations of Luhrmann and his team, the stylistic excesses and visual flair of the piece take center stage and dominate our attention. Catherine Martin's showpiece set is the grand ballroom of the Capulet Mansion, a massive and opulent temple to the god of avarice. Dominating the room is an immense painting of the Madonna and Child, in hues of gold and crimson. Flanking the central marble staircase are faux-Roman pillars, decorated with gilded cherubim and foreboding, eyeless masks, molded into frozen, glittery smiles. Golden statues of mermaids blowing tritons serve as lamp fixtures at the foot of the stairs. A giant, gilded two-story candelabrum, supported by a replica of the Three Graces, illuminates the room. Mirrors in ornate frames and elaborate oil paintings bedeck the walls and the Capulet herald, a baroque, stylized cat bearing the words "virtue," "honor," "Dios," and "fuerza" is inlaid in the floor.

The two gangs are resplendent in their tribal colors: the Montagues in lush Hawaiian shirts, the Capulets dressed in ornamental and expensive Dolce and Gabbana–inspired haute couture and engraved jewelry. All are adorned with ornate guns. When the two gangs clash, hurling insults and brandishing weapons, the tempo heightens along with the heated exchanges.

"Let's talk about that cinematic language. You get a lot of people saying, 'Oh my god, you change style every five minutes. How MTV!' Well, have you ever seen a Hindi movie? Please. That idea of low comedy, one minute a song, then *Rebel Without a Cause*, is aligned with Shakespeare's need to keep changing style, to keep clarity, to keep surprising the audience, to keep ahead of them. Is it more visual than Shakespeare? Absolutely. On the Elizabethan stage, people wore last year's fashions and got up and declaimed. Two comic actors came up—'allo, 'allo, 'allo—and got them laughing. Then a boy would come out in a dress as Juliet. It was funny. The play is meant to be funny. For that reason we cut a third of it, as it is visual description. Things which you cannot see: 'But soft, what light through yonder window breaks?' There was no light breaking from yonder window; it was daytime. So you had to say it. Our cinematic language is just the way we tell it. That's what changes, not the story I hope."

What was the wildest Shakespeare you've ever seen? "A lot of wild stuff doesn't work. It becomes about being groovy for the sake of being groovy. We have in Australia somebody who I think is a genius, and that's the theatre director Neil Armfield. He did a production of *Twelfth Night*, which went on to be, sort of, a film. I remember going to the theater—I was at NIDA at the time—and I was, like, 'Yeah Shakespeare's good, but hey, it's hard work.' His *Twelfth Night* was set in Club Med and there was a Latin band playing and champagne was being given out to the audience. I thought, 'This is good already.' And the music was building, and then, suddenly, bang! It goes dark. A door opens. There is a slash of white light and this guy comes out, Robert Grubb in a white suit, and he goes, 'If music be the food of life—play on.' Bang! The band starts up again and from that moment I was focused. Then after two hours it finished. We were, like, 'Let's do that again!' It was like people were speaking with their own language, using their own accents and bringing the language to themselves. So you just realized: take a great story and convert it into a way in which the audience can receive it. That was absolutely influential on me. No question. That had a sensational effect on me."

Romeo + Juliet is a story about love. What is your idea of love? Is love not possible? "I believe in love. Sounds like a song, but I do. All my works have essentially been about some degree of love. It may be a word, but in truth it's a profound emotion that is, in your body and your veins, chemical. Do I believe in the extraordinary, passionate mad things people will do for love? Yes. Is young love a lethal and dangerous drug, in a world of learned hate, where you are being told to hate someone because of their name or skin color? Do I believe in that primary myth? Absolutely I do. Am I telling it in an offhanded way to disarm people? Yes. But I do ultimately hope that you are moved by that tragedy."

Do you think love is the same now as it was at the time the play was written? "Yes. I think everything human is the same at all times. I don't think the human condition changes. The conditions around us change, but what makes us human beings does not change. You see it in his other plays. I know *Hamlet*. I know so many thirty-three-year-olds going round saying, 'I don't know—what am I gonna do, man? What's the point of living on past thirty-three?' The genius of Shakespeare is not his stories. He did not write *Romeo and Juliet*, he stole it, a long poem that was based on an Italian novella. He stole it, but his genius is his understanding of the human condition and his ability with words."

Despite the problems of working in Mexico, Luhrmann states emphatically that he wouldn't swap a day they spent in Mexico for anything in the world. The shoot lingered months longer than anticipated. A hurricane wiped out the set. Everyone succumbed to various illnesses. Shooting shut down for a week while Luhrmann had a temperature of 110. Then there was the kidnapping. "The hair and make-up person, Aldo Signoretti, who worked with Fellini, was kidnapped. We paid three hundred US dollars to get him back; I thought rather a bargain. The bandidos rang up and said, 'For three hundred dollars you can have him back.' So Maurizio, who is about this high, goes down clutching the money to outside the hotel, holds it up, chucks them the bag and they threw Aldo out of the car and broke his leg.

"So we had adventures. It was an incredible quest. It wasn't a walk in the park and the fact that the kids did what they did and put up with what they did was amazing. The reason the film is like it is, is that we embraced everything that happened. For example, Mercutio dies in that storm. That was the hurricane that came and blew our sets away. The wide shots, which you could never get, I asked the guys if the cameras could handle them. We got out and did the wides and caught the storms then we came back and did the close-ups with wind machines. For a budget like ours, you can't achieve that short of massive CGI."

Were there any aspects of your vision that weren't achieved? "Yeah, 50 percent of it. I know a very famous director and he says you get about 50 percent of what you do. Maybe not even 50 percent. I think the execution of that was maybe half of what I was hoping for. But that's always the way. You never get anywhere near what you set out to do. Then it gets kind of taken away from you. You never are happy. I don't think you ever say, 'Oh, it's absolutely perfect. Don't touch a frame.' I can't even look at it now. You see it a lot of times and you just want everything to be better. That's just the way it is."

Baz on the Bard

Peter Malone / 1997

From *Eureka Street* 7, no. 2 (March 1997). Reprinted with permission of the author.

Peter Malone: How did you manage to get *Romeo + Juliet* off the ground, especially with the backing of a major Hollywood studio?

Baz Luhrmann: It was an incredibly difficult film to get made. After *Strictly Ballroom*, we were offered all kinds of possibilities. We spent a long time away from making a film. We did other things: operas, the 1993 Australian Labor Party election launch, a *Vogue* magazine layout, and so on. Our philosophy has always been that we think up what we need in our life, choose something creative that will make that life fulfilling, and then follow that road. With *Romeo + Juliet*, what I wanted to do was to look at the way in which Shakespeare might make a movie of one of his plays if he was a director. How would he go about doing it?

We don't know a lot about Shakespeare, but we do know he would make a "movie" movie. He was a player. We know about the Elizabethan stage and that he was playing for three thousand drunken punters, from the street sweeper to the Queen of England, and that his competition was bear-baiting and prostitution. So he was a relentless entertainer and a user of incredible devices and theatrical tricks to create something of meaning and tell a story.

That was what we wanted to do. We were interested in that experience. It wasn't that some genius at the studio rang up and said, "Do a funky MTV-style Shakespeare and wipe the floor with all the other pictures. Go to number one and get all the kids in." That was not the case.

Basically it was "No, no, no!" But because I had made a film about ballroom dancing and it had grossed $80 million, I was in a first-look deal. I said, "Look, don't say yes. Just give me a few thousand dollars." I rang up Leonardo DiCaprio, whom I consider to be an incredibly important part of actually getting the film made, and he agreed to fly to Sydney, using his own money. I mean, this was a kid who's been offered the incomes of small countries! We did an initial workshop, did more script work. He flew down again and, with local actors, we created this workshop; and when they saw him (in the fight scene) get out of the car in a suit and come up and say, "Tybalt, the reason that I have to love thee doth much excuse the appertaining rage to such a greeting. Villain am I none; therefore farewell; I see thou knowest me not," they went, "Oh, yeah, we get it. They're kind of like gangs. Yeah, that could work. Gangs, that's good, that's good."

So then the executives said, "Alright, we'll give him enough money to get to production." It was sort of a war of attrition and, eventually, got to a point where they said, "Look, just give him a cheque." And, then it was, you know, "See ya!" After which we had the problems of making it. It was an enormously difficult shoot: storms, sickness, and kidnappings.

PM: In Mexico?
BL: Pre-production was all done here in Australia and all the development. Then we pre-produced in Canada and shot in Mexico. We did most of the post-production in Australia: all the sound was done here in Melbourne at Soundfilm, all the optical effects here at Complete Post. So, it's technically a Canadian-Australian co-production distributed by 20th Century Fox. But, in reality, it's my team. At a certain point, I was flying sixteen Australians, DOP, producer, editor, costume designer, production designer, music guys, assistants, choreographer, special effects, sound, etc., to North America.

So, to answer the question: it was very hard to convince them. Once I'd done so, though, they were fantastic, but kind of like, "Look, you know, he does these weird things, they seem to work. This one won't, of course. But let's let him make this and when it turkeys, he'll be ready to do *Jingle All the Way*. He'll be begging us to let him do Arnie's next picture!"

Hollywood! People have many wrong ideas about Hollywood: firstly, it's much worse than *The Player*, much more bizarre. In fact it's a community in the desert, made up of people from all over the world, the best people from all over the world. Now, what normally happens with the internationals—and most players in Hollywood are internationals—is that they are hired with their producer and they pick up American teams. But one of my non-negotiables is that I work with my team: we work together, we are a team, we are an environment. Since the success of *Romeo + Juliet*, I have an unprecedented deal where working with my team is actually ensconced in it.

Do they reject us? No, they don't. I mean, half of the best people in Hollywood are Australians! I think a huge percentage of the DPs are Australians.

PM: The preparation?
BL: I wanted to do Shakespeare makes a film, *Romeo and Juliet.* The first thing to identify was a way of conveying the notions of the piece, release the language, and set it in a particular world. You couldn't set it in the real world because it would then become a social exploration of Miami or LA or Sydney, wherever. So we decided to create a world and that world was created from meticulous research of the Elizabethan world. For example, a social reality for the Elizabethan world was that everyone carried a weapon. Then we found a way of interpreting that in the twentieth century. There were schools of sword fighting; they became schools of gunfighting. Only gentlemen would carry weapons, not the poor. Suddenly you had a place that looked a bit like South America, but it also looked like Miami. We picked the dominant culture. Whatever you say, the dominant culture in the western world is American, especially through the media.

So we created a world: it's American, Latin, it looks a bit like South America, it feels a bit like Mexico, it feels somewhat like Miami, but, ultimately, it's Verona Beach, which is ultimately a universal city. Now, that is not so out of keeping with what Shakespeare did. He never went to Verona. He created his mythical city. But really it was London, dressed up as a hot version of London. So that was that part of the process.

Then we spent a lot of time researching the Elizabethan stage and transformed that into cinematic ideas. We went to Miami, which we chose because it's a really good place that condenses American or contemporary Western images. It is both culturally mixed and very violent, almost an armed society.

Out of that research, we wrote the screenplay. We came back and did a series of workshops with actors in Sydney. Then I got (cinematographer) Don McAlpine in. For free, he got a video camera and, for a week, we shot scenes with Leonardo: the fight scene, the death scene.

We are noted for doing a ludicrous amount of preparation. And we are noted for a ridiculous kind of research, but this is what we like to do: the act of making must make your life rich. It's got to be interesting and fulfilling and educational and take you on a journey. They're the choices we make.

The only sacrifice you have to make is fiscally. To have been very, very wealthy would have been easy after *Strictly Ballroom.* I'm not poor, but the kind of wealth that I know others have is not ours because we choose to do the Bard in a funky manner. That's more interesting than doing *Jingle All the Way*! But also, we're not for hire; we never have been. Freedom is worth something.

PM: So it's not just a relocation of *Romeo and Juliet* to a different city and it's not even an updating, bringing it into the twentieth century?

BL: I think what we're doing is William Shakespeare's play of *Romeo and Juliet* and interpreting it in twentieth-century images to release the language and to find a style for communicating it to a contemporary audience. Now, you might say, "Well, that's a bit of a mouthful," and it is. I got a card from Kenny Branagh saying, "Love the film and what a great thing for our *Hamlet*, because it's opening up an audience too." I love the Laurence Olivier productions and I think Kenneth Branagh is fantastic.

But some critics have left the film and said, "The accent is completely wrong. How dare you do it that way? It's embarrassing." The truth of the matter is that Shakespeare wrote these plays for (the equivalent of) an American accent. Americans speak a version of Elizabethan sound. With a rolled R in there, you would basically have the Elizabethan stage sound. I worked with Sir Peter Hall on this. He does the accent. He came to Canada and did it for me. Now, that doesn't mean we should do all Shakespeare in the Elizabethan sound. But round-vowelled English pronunciation is a fashion. It was just the right way or the right fashion or the right device for a particular time to tell or reveal the play for that time.

To have Leonardo DiCaprio asking, "Is she a Capulet?" in a southern Californian accent is not too far from the Elizabethan stage sound; it is just another way of revealing the language. So it's not wrong. It's not the only way, but it's not wrong. I had a great triumph when two Californian academics—after a kind of Mr. Ex-English teacher "I've become a local critic of the *Boulder Daily News*" declared the film was an outrage—stood up and said, "Well, in fact, Mr. Luhrmann is correct about this."

I mean, the truth is this: one thing we know is that we don't know much about Shakespeare, but he was sure as hell focused on box office and he is not displeased that he's packing the houses. I know! William Shakespeare was an actor in a company that was competing with another. All they cared about was packing the house. Who's worried that we put rock music in? For their information, here's the news: he put popular songs of the time in his shows because it was a good way of telling a story!

In terms of liberating the language, the cast had a strong sense of the rhythm, the poetry. Dustin Hoffman did Shylock in *The Merchant of Venice* on Broadway, but he lacked a sense of the verse rhythms. Do you know why I think that happened? Dustin Hoffman is a fantastic actor, but what you get there is a brand of American actor that has this reverential attitude towards the English Shakespearian style, so you get a mid-Atlantic feel. Some Americans don't use their natural sound. They adjust their sound, and they try to take on a kind of subtle interpretation of what an English actor would do with the language.

Leonardo and Claire, in their innocence, brought the language to themselves. Iambic pentameter is a natural rhythm for speaking, and thoughts beat roughly in that iambic way. And they were able to find rhythm without it becoming a signpost.

There are different styles that the other actors use because they're such different characters. We've got clowning characters and the parental world, which is like a bizarre acid trip. Then you've got Father Laurence, who is midway. But the kids are really human and natural, so they're the most natural.

It's not right, it's not wrong. It's wonderful to hear Laurence Olivier say, "Now, is the winter of our discontent." And it's fantastic to hear Kenny Branagh chomp it a bit more like the Midlands sound. It's also great to hear Leonardo DiCaprio in those soft Californian sounds say, "Tybalt, the reason I have to love you. . . ."

PM: The visual style helped liberate the language and break down the barriers?

BL: It actually isn't visual style. Even on the Elizabethan stage they wore their day clothes. When it came to doing the balcony scene, they would find a usual device to free and clarify story and language.

It is true that we are intensely visual, and our intense visual language has to be freeing, not oppressing. We make pictures. Cinema is like opera, strangely. That's why cinema directors do a lot of opera and vice-versa, but not necessarily plays. They are the synthesis of the visual, the plastic, the written, the acted, the audible, the audio arts, synthesising all those things into one singular statement. There is no rule. If someone says that there's only one way to do it, that they've got the book and that theirs is The Way, you know they're talking crap because stories do not change. But the way you tell them has to be a product of the times. I'd call my book about my work, *The Way I Tell It*, but in the telling, the visual representation is a good 50 percent of that.

PM: On the visuals: you have a great number of Catholic statues and images.

BL: We shot in Mexico and Mexico is very, very, very Catholic with Catholic iconography everywhere. The giant statue of Jesus in the middle of the city—that is, Mexico City—is an electronic addition. All the iconography was about the fact of the plot point that, when you marry, it is in the eyes of God. Families can't pull the couple apart. So the slightly-on-the-edge priest says, "But, actually, if you do get married, the families can't do anything about it; and it's a way of forcing them to stop running around killing each other." It's a key plot point in the play, but it's very weak dramatically unless you have the audience believing that no-one questions religion, or the existence of God, or the power of Jesus Christ.

So when Juliet says, "No, if thy love be honorable, thy purpose marriage," Romeo could not say, "Look, you don't have to get married to have sex." There's no argument about the fact that they existed in a religious context in terms of their thinking and beliefs. So it turned out like an Italian/Mexican/South American location. I mean, when you're in Mexico, religion is absolutely wrapped up with politics. This Mediterranean, Hispanic piety is strong, as in the shrine in Juliet's room with so many statues of Mary, so many candles. Even the seedy apothecary has holy cards on his counter.

There's a lot of the iconography there and it's on the weapons as well. Now, some can say that's sacrilegious. No-one has, actually—it's been a bit of a surprise—but the truth is that that's an interpretation of religion in our societies. You can still have an armed society like Bosnia, where everyone's running around claiming they uphold Christian notions, or Mexico, where it's all very Catholic, and yet you go into a restaurant and people are holding guns.

In Elizabethan times, a lot of that iconography was put upon weapons of war, and I've always thought that's very disturbing. So it's not a judgment or an analysis of any kind of religion; it's about saying that everyone has to have a belief in a certain set of rules.

PM: And the cross on Father Laurence's back?

BL: Well, Father Laurence is very important but, actually, in the play, he's a bit of an idiot. You remember that the Elizabethan world was slashing away at Catholicism. The good news is that just because he's a priest doesn't make him God; he's a human being. I think Father Laurence is a great character and a good person, but he's had a struggle with the human condition himself. He's not perfect.

Our scenario was that he went off to Vietnam and was into drugs. He was tussling with his own personal dilemmas. Maybe he had a wife and a child or whatever, but he went back to the church and is essentially a good person. He really wants good to be done and truly believes in the ideas of Christ and God. But he's not this guy in a white caftan who says, "I have a wonderful idea. Let's marry and all will be hunky-dory." So I was showing him to be a complex man: you know, he's a drinker. I quite like it that Spencer Tracy always played priests, but was secretly a drunk, which doesn't say he's bad. I think priests that are flawed are at least more human. If you reveal it, you're therefore truthful. You're saying, "I'm a human being. I'm not a deity." I have a problem with the viewing of priesthood as somehow above it all, as a kind of deity, as I'm sure certain churches do.

PM: Your sets? Do you ever think, "This is just too much? This is overwhelming?"
BL: Do you mean too much in terms of its effectiveness in the storytelling, or just incredibly decadent?

PM: No, just in sheer extravagance.
BL: Let me give you an extravagance. That pool: that entire outdoor pool is a set, interior built. It was made from concrete and it was filled with water. The day before we finished on the set, in a frenzy to go up to Verona Beach, they drained it and the next day there were guys with jackhammers just tearing it to pieces. It was a million-dollar pool.

It's a weird little world, filmmaking, and you do weird little things. One of the things I hate is waste, and I was not able to avoid the kind of waste I would like to avoid. Everything you see on that beach is built. There's not a palm tree or a telegraph pole on that beach that wasn't put there by us. It was a desert.

The illusion of film is fascinating and difficult, but tricky. We were able to do things in Mexico that you can't do anywhere else in the world. We had this one chopper, that big white one, but it looks as if we had an entire flotilla of choppers. You can tell the electronic ones, we're not trying to hide that too much. The military guy in the chopper in silhouette early on, sitting, pointing with a gun, that's me. We were in a Bell chopper, the camera chopper, and Don McAlpine was there with the camera, hand-holding, and I was just strapped in. We also had all these stunt guys dressed up, flying over Mexico City and hanging out of the chopper.

I'll give you an example of how surreal it all was. We're up in a chopper, flying over the desert, looking for Mantua. We see tiny little sheds. So we fly down, we land, and the wind from the chopper blades blows everything all over. The sheds the villagers were living in were cardboard boxes. Our Mexican interpreter says, "Look, we want to make a film . . . and we're going to build some things here, but we'll leave everything for you and we're going to pay you this money." They're over the moon. So we came back. We built the entire town of Mantua there, everything you see there, all those shacks, the cars, everything. They're all employed and are happy about it.

We were always finding ourselves desperately behind during the actual shoot. We got the final shot, all the trucks were leaving the next morning and, as we were heading off, they're all waving and cheering us. And the town we left behind that used to be made of cardboard is now their little town. There's a big sign there now that says Mantua. That's pretty surreal.

PM: Talking of names: why *William Shakespeare's Romeo + Juliet?*
BL: Things are marketed very intensely in the US. Because it was all very modern and because it was one of many *Romeo and Juliet*s—even Shakespeare stole the story from other sources—with the way marketing minds work, it would be, "Let's just flog it as a kind of funky-looking movie called *Romeo and Juliet* and not mention Shakespeare." But by forcing them to put the name William Shakespeare in there, no matter what they did to it, there was no question that it was the play.

Not only is it the text, but the 1968 Zeffirelli version, which everyone thinks is faithful to the original language, actually has additional dialogue and changes the text: from "Do with their death bury their parents' strife . . ." to "Doth with their death . . ." I'm not criticising that, because I think it's a gorgeous production. But we are textually more accurate. We have cut about a third, under a half, which is probably normal. Zeffirelli cut half the text too.

Actors love Shakespeare because it's like giving them a sports car. They have a lot to say, and actors like to talk, God knows. We had a meticulous rehearsal process, and they really dug it. There's no actor on that show that's not happy. Brian Dennehy had about three lines. He's a terrific stage actor. I just said to him, "Look, I really need someone who could really believe he's Leonardo's father, and someone with real credibility who has good craft."

PM: You bring Shakespeare to the people. Was it a surprise that it turned out that way, that your film appears to have introduced many Americans, at least, to Shakespeare?

BL: Being number one was a surprise to everyone. Being number one in America is like saying, "I don't care what it is, I want it," to the industry. It killed *Sleepers*, a $70 million film with Robert De Niro, Brad Pitt, and Dustin Hoffman. In a town where "What do you mean, Shakespeare's number one? How come you didn't tell me about it?" that means a lot. So yes, I did want to take it back to where it began, and I did want it to be for everybody. It was for everybody.

PM: With such box office you'd almost be subject to a deity principle now, wouldn't you?

BL: More the alchemy principle, I think. What we've done in our two sorties is turn lead to gold. To understand means gold so, therefore, we must understand something about the audience that the studio people don't. Frankly, no-one knows anything, and those that do what we do are only paid because they have a better instinct than others. They don't know. I don't really know. I do know what I want to see up on the screen, and that we had the audacity and the guts and the energy to put it there, to sustain the fight to get it done.

So what has that left me with? Well, I was certainly offered higher cash deals, much more lucrative deals, by other studios. But Fox embraced the notion that I wanted to work from Australia and that I work with a large team in an idiosyncratic way. The truth about all of that is that what we do is tell stories. And what we have purchased, or won, is the freedom to think something up and do it.

Postscript: The Melbourne *Herald-Sun* of January 1, 1997, reported that, over the four days after Christmas, *Romeo + Juliet* topped the box office with $A2,277,014 while *Daylight* took $A2,235,000. Baz Luhrmann is quoted: "We feel very proud that an idea launched in Australia has been embraced so wholeheartedly and I know Shakespeare will be happy to hear that he outgrossed Sylvester Stallone."

Shakespeare in the Cinema:
A *Cineaste* Interview

Gary Crowdus / 1998

From *Cineaste*'s special "Shakespeare in the Cinema" issue, 24, no. 1 (December 1998): 48–55. Reprinted by permission of *Cineaste*, www.cineaste.com.

Luhrmann's comments extracted from a symposium that also includes Peter Brook, Sir Peter Hall, Richard Loncraine, Oliver Parker, Roman Polanski, and Franco Zeffirelli. For their invaluable assistance, the editors would like to extend their thanks to Corinne Beaver, Maria Apodiacos, Paul Watters, Moragh Darby, Isabelle Dassonvile, and Francesca Pispisa.

In order to gain insights into the aesthetic considerations and working methods Baz Luhrmann brought to bear on *William Shakespeare's Romeo + Juliet* (1996), we posed several questions to him.

Cineaste: It is almost always necessary to make cuts and other changes in the text when cinematically adapting a Shakespeare play. What is your own philosophy or strategy for making cuts, for updating antiquarian or obscure words, or for rewriting or rearranging scenes?

Baz Luhrmann: Our philosophy in adapting *Romeo and Juliet* for the screen was to reveal Shakespeare's lyrical, romantic, sweet, sexy, musical, violent, rude, rough, rowdy, rambunctious storytelling through his richly invented language. Consequently, our specific strategy was to avoid changing or adding words. We were adamant that we should maintain the color and taste of the actual words even to the extent of the "thee" and "thou."

Setting the story in the contemporary world of urban gangs allowed us to put Shakespeare's inventive usage to work as a dexterous and ornate street rap. This game allowed us to justify all words even when the actual meaning was not immediately apparent. For example, in a contemporary film, a character in a gang may say something is "Bad" when in fact the meaning is "Good." In a similar fashion Tybalt says to Mercutio, "Thou consortest with Romeo," with "consortest" bearing a sexual inference. Therefore, we see that if the intention behind the word is clear then the meaning will be too.

Where we took significant liberty was in restructuring and cutting. We felt it was important to serve Shakespeare's ultimate goal of strong storytelling. He had to arrest the attention of a very noisy, disparate, savage yet honest audience, not unlike at your local cinema. To facilitate this, he used all the devices at his disposal, the clash of lowbrow comedy with high tragedy, the use of popular song (pop music), etc. Similarly, we developed a specific cinematic language for *Romeo + Juliet* that transformed all of these devices into cinematic equivalents in order to achieve the same goal with our noisy, disparate, savage yet honest audience.

Cineaste: Should the actors in a Shakespearean film be classically trained stage actors, preferably with previous experience in Shakespeare's plays, or do you believe that any good actor, with proper direction, can perform Shakespearean roles?

BL: I am always surprised by how many people relate to the nineteenth-century notion of Shakespeare or the 1930s fashion of Received Pronunciation as the so-called "classical style." We spent a year researching the Elizabethan stage, focusing on the linguistic work of Anthony Burgess and holding discussions with people like Sir Peter Hall. It became clear that Received Pronunciation, that is, the round vowel sounds of Olivier and Gielgud or "Voice Beautiful" as it is known, is a relatively new fashion.

It is fair to say that if the Elizabethan actor were to perform for us today both his sound and style of acting would quite likely shock our notion of "Classical." The sound of his language would be more guttural with a heavy rolled "r." As Anthony Burgess pointed out, it was closer to the sound of the American accent than "Voice Beautiful." Regardless of an actor's formal training, or the lack of it, the simple answer is: whatever makes a particular production at a particular moment in time work for that particular audience is "right."

Cineaste: What is your view of the proper presentation of Shakespeare's verse in a film? Should it be delivered differently on screen than on the stage? Do you attempt to preserve the poetic and musical quality of the blank verse, or do you think it's more important for the actors to achieve a more naturalistic delivery that will not seem so alien to the ears of contemporary moviegoers, most of whom are not theatergoers?

BL: One of the great things about Shakespeare's text is its musicality and rhythm. The fact is the actor learns so much about what they are doing and saying from the rhythm itself. I do believe that this rhythm should, where possible, be maintained. As far as the way in which it's delivered, again it is whatever works for a particular situation. There is no reason why an actor cannot deliver the line in a natural style while maintaining the underlying meter.

Cineaste: Do cinematic techniques offer new possibilities for exploring and presenting Shakespeare (such as dealing with subtext)? Do you believe that a film version of a Shakespeare play demands a more fully developed interpretation of the play on the part of the film director than a stage presentation does?

BL: I don't believe the demands on the stage director are more or less great than those on the film director. Having worked in both film and theater, I have found the interpretation of a text needs equal thought and development regardless of the medium. Obviously when cinematic language can replace stage convention, it may help the telling. However, this is not specific to Shakespeare.

Cineaste: Is it possible for film versions of Shakespeare to be too visual, too realistic? Do you prefer to utilize fully the cinema's capacity for verisimilitude, or do you prefer to maintain a certain abstraction in the sets and decor? Why?

BL: Is it possible to do a film version of Shakespeare that is "too visual, too realistic"? Too much for whom? The concept that there is a set of Shakespearean rules with a foreword by the great man himself, with chapter headings such as "too visual," "too realistic," "over-abstraction, under-abstraction: the use of cryptic symbolism in the minimalist style" is not only ludicrous but irrelevant.

Little factual information about Shakespeare has survived. However, we do get the sense that he liked to "pack the house"; was big on laughter; big on tears; loved the pun, the bawdy gag, the odd song, and a spectacular "blood and guts" sword fight. Above all, he would delight, amaze, and captivate with words while managing at the same time to draw a curtain back and reveal the human condition. In any case, I think in any film, whether Shakespeare or not, the visual language has to reveal, support, and clarify the storytelling.

Cineaste: Is it important for a director of a Shakespearean film to be knowledgeable about the history, the culture, and the cosmology of the Elizabethan world in which Shakespeare wrote his plays?

BL: As with any story, if you don't understand the world in which the text was generated and if you don't have an absolute, totally, and utterly thorough understanding of the history, culture, and cosmology of everything about that world, then you are interpreting the text in a vacuum.

Cineaste: What is your view of filming historically updated versions of Shakespeare's plays as opposed to period presentations?

BL: Having directed Shakespeare in theater, opera, and film, it's never been a question of, is there a right or a wrong method. One must simply address an audience at a particular moment in time and attempt to reveal the greater richness of the particular idea or story. Whether you do an unbelievably accurate Elizabethan version, performed on a bare stage, in the middle of the day to four thousand mostly drunk punters with the female roles played by adolescent boys in drag and spoken in a virtually incomprehensible accent, or any other interpretation, it is correct if it reveals the heart of the story and engages and awakens the audience to the material.

Cineaste: Producing a Shakespearean film is usually referred to as "popularizing" Shakespeare for a mass moviegoing audience. What is your view? What sort of compromises does such "popularization" involve?

BL: It is almost embarrassing to me when people start talking about Shakespeare as if his intention was not to be popular or as if he was a storyteller, playwright, poet, and actor who was not interested in the widest possible audience. Do we think Shakespeare would be turning in his grave because he beat Sylvester Stallone at the opening weekend of *Romeo + Juliet*? I don't think so.

Are we trying to say that a man who had to play to four thousand punters a day and to every kind of person from the street sweeper to the Queen of England wouldn't be interested in being successful in the multiplexes? At what time was Shakespeare only interested in playing to a small elite? I don't understand that notion. It seems that the antithesis of everything Shakespeare stood for is to treat his text as high culture.

Cineaste: Are you encouraged by the present vogue for Shakespearean films? Will such a trend make it easier for you to make another

Shakespearean film? Do you have a Shakespeare play in mind that you would like to film?

BL: When I was young I was mostly exposed to bad productions and found Shakespeare impenetrable. Then one day I experienced the stage production of *Twelfth Night* by Neil Armfield and suddenly a curtain was pulled back. Shakespeare's storytelling was suddenly relevant and I realized what I'd been missing out on. In answering your question, I find it encouraging that many different directors are taking on the responsibility of revealing the richness of these plays to audiences who, like myself, may have missed out, while at the same time reawakening old fans through fresh tellings.

Concerning *Romeo + Juliet*, I expect my interpretation to be written off as "old hat" one day soon and replaced by a new cinema version. Maybe it will be a very accurate Elizabethan interpretation—who knows? What is really important is, as Benjamin Britten once said, if a story is true then there will be many different productions in many different places and it will go on and on. My own view is that truly great storytelling defies time, geography, and the so-called rules of right and wrong. The proof of its worth is that it lives on.

Baz Luhrmann

Elsie M. Walker / 2000

From *Conversations with Directors: An Anthology of Interviews from Literature/Film Quarterly*, edited by Elsie M. Walker and David T. Johnson (Lanham, Maryland: The Scarecrow Press, 2008), 300–10. Reprinted by permission.

Baz Luhrmann has made three films to date: *Strictly Ballroom* (1991), *William Shakespeare's Romeo + Juliet* (1996), and *Moulin Rouge!* (2001). These films, marketed as "the Red Curtain Trilogy," have already established Luhrmann's status as one of the foremost Australian auteurs. They are united through their combination of theatricality and cinematic complexity, the audaciously postmodern exuberance of their mise-en-scènes, their emphasis on musical eclecticism (though only *Moulin Rouge!* is identified as a musical), and their emphasis on self-conscious storytelling. The films are also united in the ways they self-consciously and paradoxically combine excessive materialism and self-evident commercial imperatives with nostalgic, high Romanticism. *Romeo + Juliet* is one of the most financially successful Shakespearean adaptations to date,[1] yet the film itself applauds belief in the fundamental value of love "beyond the market."[2]

This interview took place on July 9, 2000, when I met Luhrmann at the headquarters of his production company Bazmark: the House of Iona in Sydney, Australia. He had finished post-production work on *Moulin Rouge!* for the day: the interview was at approximately 10:00 at night. When I arrived at the luminously lit House of Iona I found myself standing before two enormous iron gates. Given my short stature, I was intimidated by the intercom system that was positioned above my eye-line. I was about to stand on tip-toe to announce my arrival when the gates silently, mysteriously, and slowly opened before me. I realized that someone unseen had seen my approach. There was a pale round face at the window: the face of, as I learned later, Luhrmann's assistant, affectionately known as "Dubsy." I made it down a cobbled path, like something from *The Wizard of Oz* (1939), lined with extraordinary foliage and a prominent palm tree. Dubsy opened the enormous front door and escorted me through a main entrance hall with a massive staircase reminiscent of the one featured in the Capulet mansion of Luhrmann's *Romeo + Juliet*. He then led me to a room with bright red walls, velvet-covered sofas with splendidly detailed cushions (like props in *Moulin Rouge!*), and walls featuring shiny awards for *Strictly Ballroom* and *Romeo + Juliet*. I was dwarfed by the splendor of the room which was itself like a kind of set. Luhrmann then entered, wearing an immaculate brown suit and a Yankees baseball cap. The sheer opulence of the House of Iona, the almost performative display of objects within it, along with the apparently studied paradox of Luhrmann's dress (the informal accessory with a suit) led me to expect a performance from Luhrmann that would make it difficult for me to get the candid, unrehearsed responses I wanted. While Luhrmann made versions of several comments I had already read or heard in other interviews, he was exceptionally generous in his excitable and exciting responses to my questions about *Romeo + Juliet*, particularly questions concerned with tonal complexity and music which had not been discussed in previous interviews.

My transcript of the interview reflects Luhrmann's multi-clause, rapid-fire, and multi-directional speaking rhythm. His speech seemed almost as quick as the editing of his films. He described various processes involved in the making of *Romeo + Juliet*: selling the idea to financial backers, pitching the film for a contemporary young audience, self-consciously translating Shakespeare's words in visual and contemporary terms, making a stylistically ambitious film reflective of Shakespearean tonal complexity, and structuring the film in terms of music.

Elsie M. Walker: I think the academic world was quite slow to appreciate your film and quite distrusting of it—perhaps because of its popularity.
Baz Luhrmann: I think that's probably true. And much more so in the United States than in England. Because the Americans by their very nature are very suspicious of Shakespeare. Because there's a massive pretension there that they fear, they're insecure about it. And particularly the academics tend to revere backwards to their most loved production that they saw in the 1960s or some time. You're right there, although I know I did a show recently, for the BBC or ITV. . . .

EW: The Southbank Show?
BL: Yes. I know there was a guy from Oxford University and I thought he had a surprisingly clear take on it.

EW: I remember that, at the centenary conference about Shakespeare on screen (in 1999), your film was being spoken of as a landmark production whereas people were suspicious of it before then.[3] And I was wondering why you think there might be that kind of shift.
BL: I think, firstly, that with any film, when you release it, you know you have to go through this big mechanism called marketing. First of all, I could spend hours talking about the history of the film. But just so you have an understanding: it wasn't like I said, after making *Strictly Ballroom* (and I have a five-year quite extraordinary deal with Fox so I can sort of make what I want), "I want to do a funky *Romeo and Juliet.*" I didn't say "funky Romeo and Juliet," but when I said I wanted to do a Shakespeare in modern dress they didn't go, like, "What a great idea, that is a great idea, you know we must do that, that's amazing." That photo of Leonardo [DiCaprio, on the wall] was taken here in Sydney a year and a half before I made the film. So D. came down here and we really had to make a video version of it to convince the studio to give us the money. So, what I'm saying is, having invested what they saw as an enormous amount for a Shakespeare—because mainstream studios have not tended to do Shakespeare, independent studios have—then selling it became a thing of absolutely nailing your audience. So they sold it very precisely as a youth market picture and as a sort of MTV *Romeo and Juliet.* Now, this is how distant that is from our process. Our process, my process, was: I wanted to investigate the myth and the fact of Shakespeare and I wanted to tell the Shakespearean piece, a Shakespearean piece, in the way in which perhaps Shakespeare would today if he were here directing a film. And every choice we made was based on two years of meticulous research about the Elizabethan stage. So, for example, on the Elizabethan stage, as you would well know, Shakespeare would use very low comedy and cut it with very high tragedy and popular song.

EW: Wild juxtapositions.
BL: All the time. See you've got to remember that a thirteen-year-old boy was playing Juliet. So, you've already got this very heightened deal. Now you'd have two stand-up comics come out and say, "Do you bite your thumb at me, sir, oh I do bite my thumb at you."

EW: That's a scene [the first fight scene from *Romeo and Juliet*] that can really fall flat in stage productions and on film. And you did something quite incredible with it, with all the western allusions and the action movie conventions. . . .

BL: Again, it comes back to Shakespeare because . . . Shakespeare would do *anything*. He wasn't a thematic teller. He didn't think, "Well, I'm doing a tragedy, so it must all be in a certain color and a certain rhythm." He said . . . the audience, an audience as you would well know of four thousand in a city of four hundred thousand, next to the bear-baiting and the prostitution, who are mainly drunk, incredibly violent, and unbelievably noisy. He had to shut them up with jokes and *then* hit them with an emotional twist. Our cinema audience is much closer to his audience than an audience in a theater today. They're a rowdy, noisy bunch who aren't going to be easily won over. So, we had to use the same aggression of device to shut them up. So, for example, we relate to many movies that they would know, subconsciously, like we were specifically quoting a Morricone spaghetti western in the beginning, and then when Romeo's out in the desert we're specifically quoting *Giant* [1956], the James Dean [film]. The way in which Leonardo looks is a combination of Kurt Cobain and James Dean. So, we specifically quoted that in the style. The world of the film . . . we spent a good year researching social and economic realities of the Elizabethan world, then translated them into a tear-sheet of twentieth-century images. So, we took an image that said religion and politics are mixed up together, so you get the giant Christian cross and religious symbols, a world where the wearing of a weapon gave you status—suddenly it starts to look like a South American city. We went then to Miami . . . we actually started in Verona oddly enough. We then went to England, did the English research there, then went to Miami, because Miami, for us, was the closest kind of city to an Elizabethan city. Hot.

EW: And then you ended up in Mexico.

BL: Finally shooting in Mexico. But if you think of that environment, even though it's a heightened world—you've got a hot, sexy environment, full of religion, signs, and symbols, and Miami, where there is a schism, 50 percent of the population speaks Spanish as their first language, and there's a gang temperature there.

So to answer your first question, I think initially, just by the publicity of it, academics thought, "Oh, Shakespeare-lite" or "funky Shakespeare."

When they finally had a look at the work . . . if you know anything about Shakespeare, you had to start to register that a great deal of meticulous research . . . that the ideas of execution came directly from the Elizabethan stage.

EW: I suppose nowadays people in theaters tend to behave a bit like a congregation rather than, as you say, the rambunctious crowd of . . .
BL: Well, Shakespeare wrote for everyone, from the street sweeper to the Queen of England: they all had to get it. And it's why I revere him so much as a storyteller because he was dealing with a supremely alive, real audience, who had to be absolutely and totally arrested into the story. They didn't come quietly.

EW: But many of them were presumably also attuned to a particular way of speaking, a particularly condensed way of speaking. In connection with the language, I wanted to ask you how you made cuts to stick to the "two hour's traffic." And, how did you go about making the text visual? . . . Because it seems to me that you incorporate so many of the images that Shakespeare conjures textually. So can you describe that process?
BL: It's a good question. One thing, remember this: first, language. One of the great criticisms we sometimes get is, oh, but you know, you've got people gabbling in American accents and, you know, Latin accents. But remembering that when Shakespeare was acting people probably spoke more like that, with a very round sound. And I think it's Anthony Burgess—he's the most interesting person on this (I think he's a linguistic person)—[who explores] the concept that the Americas were settled by Elizabethans and, in fact, I think it's irrelevant whether it's an American accent or whatever: the truth is you probably couldn't understand the play if it was performed in its original sound. But, leaving that aside, what most critics get obsessed with is really a modern invention, the clipped R.P. [received pronunciation] "voice beautiful." So, that goes out the window. Secondly, in the cutting, one thing that Craig [Pearce] and I adhered to was that we cut and we reconfigured scenes but we kept the language. Even Zeffirelli changed the "thee" and the "thou" and he changed some words . . . there's additional dialogue. But every word in that piece is by William Shakespeare. We have reconfigured and moved and cut to compress.

The genius and the paradox of Shakespeare is that they'd come on in their basic clothes and they'd pick up a sword and go "I'm a king." And the other great thing is, why he's so cinematic in a sense, is that because there were no . . . most people's idea of great Shakespeare is nineteenth-century, you know: big sets, pantaloons, or Leslie Howard climbing up a big piece of scenery.[4]

EW: A disastrous Romeo!
BL: Disastrous but unbelievably funny, nice pond in the balcony scene, and that's about it.

EW: And the feet off the floor in the bedroom scene because of the Production Code.
BL: Anyway, the point is, having said that, Shakespeare's great success is his rhythmic scene changes—like in film. And how he does it is he'll write, "What news of the king?" "Here comes the messenger!" (and you know he's outside). He's got that massive, fast cutting already in the language, so it's about visually realizing the world, and one of the interesting examples of that is . . . maybe a digression from the questions but . . . Say, if you take the balcony scene—I mean taking the absolute truth of that scene but converting it into a modern situation—basically, he's looking up at the girl's room and he's saying, "Oh God, oh I'm so in love with Juliet, oh my God, a light's come on, oh God it is Juliet, oh my God sweet angel, if I could . . . ," and then he clambers up there and then she discovers him and then they almost touch, and it's a push-me, pull-you scene, and it would have been hilariously funny because a thirteen-year-old boy would've been saying, "Oh Romeo! Romeo!" and the nurse and all of that . . . So it's high comedy as well.

EW: But then there are accounts of really convincing, moving performances by boy actors. . . .
BL: That's nothing. I've seen a fifty-year-old man play a ten-year-old child and you weep. It's only the actor's power, but nonetheless the scene is rich in comedy and yet the beauty of their romance. And the death scene has it too, strangely. The actual moment of death, maybe that doesn't, but in the actual Shakespearean text there's a retelling of the story and there's a joke in there because they had to recount it, maybe because people left to go the bathroom or something. I think it's the Prince who says something like "you go on too long."

There's a gag in there to break the tension. So, I'd say that he uses the device anyway: of, at the most serious moments, having comedy.

EW: Which, I think, would be true of many parts of your film as well.

BL: That's a style that we utilized all the way through it, and purposely, and it's something I'm utilizing in this next film I'm doing [*Moulin Rouge!*].

EW: Can you tell me about how you sold the idea to financial backers. Did you tell them, for example, how eclectic it would be?

BL: I already was in a deal with 20th Century Fox for five years. I don't have to make films. They didn't want to do a Shakespeare: they said, "You know, we really like the idea, set it in Miami, young people great, but do you think you could do just one thing: change the language?"

EW: So how did you persuade them to keep it in?

BL: Well, I basically am a fairly persuasive chap and I brought Leonardo down and we shot a whole chunk of it. And then when they actually saw the boys get out of the cars with the guns and say, "Do you bite your thumb at me sir?" they went, "Oh, I get it, it's like gangs, it's gang language." And that's in fact what we're doing: when you've got an urban gang film, you've got someone saying, "Hey motherfucker, you're so bad," when they mean good or whatever, so that use of language [is connectable with Shakespeare]: I mean this is a man who invented one-quarter of the English language, so the extraordinary [verbal] elasticity and invention we related to street gangs and they got that very strongly. Finally, they gave in and it wasn't that much money for them: fifteen million they gave me and I ended up with twenty.

EW: So, a comparatively small production.

BL: Tiny. And it made a lot of money.

EW: Why do you think that the film spoke so deeply to the predominantly young audience?

BL: I think the piece speaks to young people anyway. All I did was find a way . . . and remember Shakespeare didn't write the story. That myth has been with us forever: youth in conflict with society, the extreme danger of absolutism, of idealistic love and youth. The great point of the piece is that if the incumbent generation propagates hate of any kind—racial hate, hate over religion, sexuality, whatever reason—it will come back on them. And the greatest loss is that you lose your children over your hate. It comes around in a circle. That is, for me, the ultimate idea in the piece.

EW: I was curious to know your take on a line of the Chorus's first speech: "Doth with their death bury their parents' strife." Did you take that as absolutely true, or did you want to cast some doubt on that? Because it seemed that the ending of the film was quite open.

BL: You're quite right. I think, traditionally, there is a scene where there is a conclusion with all the characters. But it was just rhythmically better for this film to finish with the death. And so it seemed better to say, "And of course, their death resolved the conflict?" But there is a real argument, and a genuine and a fair one that we . . . I actually shot the whole scene with the parents arriving and the priest telling the story. Finally, because of film and clarity you get, it just seemed unnecessary.

EW: An unnecessary coda.

BL: Yeah.

EW: Can I also ask you about the music in the film? Because I was interested in how you think your experience in directing opera might have influenced this film?

BL: I see music in life actually. I'm sort of with Pythagoras. I almost think the very matter from which we are made is musical and, in terms of storytelling—that's what I do, it's my work, and my life really—I see music as the great, great asset, a tool of it. But, also, I think it's a force that bonds all humanity. So it was important to find musical language. The language itself is musical, so it's important to find a musical language, a musical way of using popular music. Shakespeare used popular music on the stage, so I wanted to find a way of using popular music as a way of opening the door into the language. I'm working with the same team now except for Nellee [Hooper]. I worked with Thom Yorke of Radiohead—we all work together. He wrote "Exit Music" especially for the film. To me, all movies are a piece of music in that they have rhythm and structure and rise and fall and then you have other movements, if you like, which are the tracks within them.

EW: Can you describe the process of fitting the film to music or fitting music to the film?

BL: Traditionally, what you do in a drama is you shoot your film and then you sort of add music a bit like you add wallpaper. But we write our music into the film. So, for example, when you see the little boy singing "When Doves Cry" as a hymn, that's written in the script: "A young boy

who looks like a young Stevie Wonder sings with the choir." I write the
music into the script.

EW: So did you have Craig Armstrong's "O Verona" in your mind when
you made the film?
BL: Actually, no. To be real about that, what happened was that then
you'd have other templature music that you'd cut to, so, of course, [in
the case of] "O Verona," you don't have to be much of a musicologist
to tell that our template would've been "O Fortuna." There's been a big
problem with the Orff estate, so you couldn't get "O Fortuna" and so—I
actually worked with Marius de Vries (it was actually Maz that got that
together with Craig)—we inverted it and just created our own version of
"O Verona." But even then, for example, "Pretty Piece of Flesh" is Shakespearean text but as a kind of rap.

EW: So what kind of brief did you give these music people?
BL: They're rock 'n' roll, so it's very unusual for them to work in this way
and take so much time out. But that's just the bottom line for people
who want to work with me: they come to Australia and they live here
and work with me.

EW: So what was the rationale behind using such an eclectic soundtrack?
BL: The reason is very specific. What I like about soundtracks is they're
like mix tapes and, actually, each musical idea was specifically . . . a lot
of people put soundtracks together by basically saying, "Well, let's just
put a whole lot of groovy tracks together and we might sell some tickets
to the film." But mine are put together based on [the idea that] every
track must serve the story. So "O Verona" is clearly needed there. And
you need a track about the boys doing their thing and "Pretty Piece of
Flesh" makes sense. You want a really naïve little moment. . . . Now the
Cardigans' track had been around. . . . That song, "Love me, love me,"
becomes Juliet's theme. And then we extrapolate the set pieces through
the score, throughout the whole piece. So, for example, "Kissing You,"
the Des'ree piece which she wrote specifically for the film, becomes the
score in the balcony scene. . . .

EW: Yes, I've picked up those relationships that Craig Armstrong had
woven into the score and the various different motifs. . . .
BL: We write it exactly like an opera. It's the same thing I'm doing with

Moulin Rouge! You set up a primary theme, a song or aria, and then you thematically weave that through depending on what the action is. So, it's exactly like an opera. But remember that he [Armstrong] did it with Marius de Vries and Laura Ziffren. But he actually writes the dots.

EW: Tell me how the final film differed from your original intentions. I mean were there big surprises during filming and were there things that changed substantially during filming?

BL: Okay, they're great questions and you know time never really helps. Let me say this: on every film we make, we go through an incredibly thorough process. In fact, we've been pretty low-key about it, but I've only made two films in ten years and I spent about three years just making them, researching. Because I love researching and to live the life of the work. So, if you were to see all the early drafts, all the incarnations of it, you would be shocked and surprised by how many different developments we had. We had one version where we had mock Elizabethan ads in it and devices to try to help clarification. And some of the plotting was quite different. But if you read the very early treatment I did and then look at Craig's and my drafts, they are essentially the same idea. But there was a time, for example, when the whole scene in Mantua was set in the coast off Miami, with speedboats going forwards and back, and the coastguard arrested them. In shooting, surprises, yes . . . people got very sick . . . but one very simple change I can think of was when we first developed the film: she [Juliet] was put in a tomb, the Capulets' tomb, and people came to visit her there, in a family mausoleum. So we went to Miami and we found these fabulous mausoleums and we copied one of them. So we were down in Mexico and I kept doing the staging in the mausoleum and whichever way I looked at it—you know, people coming in, stone building, round—in an already very artificial film, it just seemed so artificial. And I just couldn't figure out why I couldn't make the scene work. I kept looking at the set, and then I realized that the problem is that mausoleums are theatrical sets. By their very nature, they're not naturalistic real rooms: they're theatrical rooms, they're stylized, like theater sets, stylized theatrical sets. So, at the same time, we found that very extraordinary church in Mexico with the Jesus on the top—it really exists. Do you know that the whole end scene was filmed in a church, a real church, and the only stipulation was that we didn't blow her head off on the altar? Because we had to shoot on the altar. So there's a tiny little trickle of CGI blood out of her, but, basically, it was shot, all of that, in a real church in Mexico City and we dressed it. So then I thought, what if they just leave her in state overnight in the church to be buried overnight? And no-one's ever questioned that. I think Romeo gets the priest, there's the chopper, and he breaks his way in. . . .

EW: But once Romeo enters the church, the noise and other characters (besides Juliet) fade away. I remember that someone asked me, "How is it that they just disappear?" But you forget about the other characters: they become temporarily unimportant. When did you decide to have Juliet wake up just after Romeo has taken the potion?
BL: Ah! That's a good question. Actually, in doing my research I found that, in the nineteenth century, they used to do lots of big re-writes.

EW: Echoing the one by David Garrick?[5]
BL: Yes, like the Garrick—she has to wake up and do a big speech. Her part wasn't big enough. It's a sort of Sarah Bernhardt.

EW: Or like Pyramus and Thisbe?!
BL: Yeah, a Pyramus and Thisbe gig, and she'd wake up and do a twenty-minute . . .

EW: I die, I die, I die!
BL: But I always thought, actually, how there was something good in that. I actually wonder if Shakespeare found it a bit hard to do too much with a thirteen-year-old boy kissing and . . . I'm sure they were extraordinary and beautiful, but probably it's harder to do. Juliet does seem to be low-key at those moments. . . . There's always a reason why they're never truly together isn't there? Maybe that's a presumption. Either way, I thought it would be great, it's the most emotional scene. He comes there, she's dead, he dies, she wakes up, she dies. So, I just thought by extending the moment there'd be this very dramatic, final realization. It compresses it doesn't it?

EW: I think if you have the full Shakespearean text, all of that happens very quickly, but if you've pared down the text it seems rhythmically right to . . .
BL: Extend that moment.

EW: Yes.

BL: So, you know, it's really a staging thing. Finally, productions are interpretations, everyone just does their own interpretation. I think that in any death moment, seeing the person that you love just before you die is a strong moment.

EW: So many people know the story already that it reinstalls the shock.
BL: I've been in audiences in LA and they've gone, "She's waking up, oh she's gonna be okay," because they don't know the ending. You'd be shocked how many kids in the US don't know the ending of *Romeo and Juliet*!

EW: So do you think you'll ever make another Shakespeare film?
BL: Maybe. . . . For the moment, I have other things that I have to attend to. Each piece comes from its own particular journey and they relate very specifically to my life and what I want to investigate or express.

Notes

1. Luhrmann's *Romeo + Juliet* was number one in its first weekend at the US box office, making over US$11 million on 1,277 screens. The film, which was made for about US$20 million, grossed over US$147 million worldwide. "Box Office Mojo" (Burbank, California), http://www.boxofficemojo.com/movies/?id=romeoandjuliet.htm (July 14, 2007).

2. I quote Catherine Belsey, who writes that love is finally "a value that remains beyond the market" (72). As Belsey writes, "The postmodern condition brings with it an incredulity towards true love," but, when it seems that everything else can be bought, love "becomes more precious than before because it is beyond price, and in consequence its metaphysical character is intensified." In postmodern culture, love is "infinitely uniquely desirable on the one hand, and conspicuously naïve on the other" (1994, 73). After all, postmodernism "repudiates the modernist nostalgia for the unpresentable, ineffable truth of things" (77). Catherine Belsey, *Desire: Love Stories in Western Culture* (Oxford: Blackwell, 1994).

3. At Shakespeare on Screen: The Centenary Conference (Mâlaga, Spain, September 21–27, 1999), there were nine separate presentations on Luhrmann's film alone.

4. The 1936 film version of *Romeo and Juliet*, directed by George Cukor, starred Leslie Howard (Romeo) and Norma Shearer (Juliet). The film came out when the Production Code (or Hays Code) was in effect and had to be obeyed if a picture was to receive the Office's "seal of approval": amongst many things, the Code forbade scenes in which a couple was in bed with more than two of their four feet off the floor.

5. Here I refer to David Garrick's now notorious, eighteenth-century adaptation of *Romeo and Juliet* (1748), which, like Luhrmann's film, has Juliet waking early in the tomb scene and makes cuts that focus more attention on the lovers throughout the play. Unlike Luhrmann, however, Garrick also added lines of his own for the lovers in the final scene.

Broadly Speaking

Sonya Voumard / 1997

From the *Sunday Age*, Melbourne, Australia, November 9, 1997. Reprinted by permission of the author.

In the late 1980s, somebody gave Baz Luhrmann some bad advice: never work with your friends. He took it against his better judgment—and the stage production he was working on flopped. "I listened and it killed me," Luhrmann recalls.

These days, even though the acclaimed director of *Strictly Ballroom* and *Romeo + Juliet* can, he says without a hint of shyness, work with anyone in the world, Luhrmann sticks primarily with his friends. His close-knit team hangs out in a grand old house in inner-Sydney's Darlinghurst where, as Luhrmann likes to put it, ideas, people, and creativity float freely from room to room.

It was in this manner that his latest quirky little project, a CD titled *Something for Everybody*, was born. Sal the secretary had been getting bad vibes about the effect the telephone music in the Luhrmann "household" was having on callers.

They were hearing tracks from the recently finished *Romeo + Juliet Volume 2* album, which contains some intense Gregorian dirges, explains Luhrmann. "Sally, whom I really trust, was saying, 'Look Baz, people are really traumatized by that music. Shouldn't we be putting on music that puts people in a positive mood?'"

Luhrmann agreed and told his team to create a CD with all the happy music they had used in their work over the past ten years. "It was a great idea and I also thought what a great Christmas present it would be," he says.

"Anton, who is the head of music here, said, 'Why don't we go in and remix just one track?' And from there we went into doing complete remixes and basically conceptualizing the fact that it's a celebration of the music we have worked on over the last ten years."

Luhrmann also sees it as being a bit like a photo album, a memoir of people he and his gang have worked with. *Something for Everybody* is a deliberately eclectic bunch of songs including "Young Hearts Run Free (Overture Mix)," a remixed version of the *Strictly Ballroom*–featured Cyndi Lauper song, "Time After Time," the "Everybody's Free (To Wear Sunscreen) Mix," which is fast becoming a Triple J cult classic [ed. Triple J is a hip FM radio station Down Under], and, finally, Holst's "Jupiter Suite," an orchestral interpretation of the hymn "Jerusalem."

Says Luhrmann, "There are these really strong, disparate bits, but they all come together as a whole. Our recognizable cinematic and theatrical language around the world is made of that because the country is made of that. In Australia more than anywhere else in the world, we are able to say that strong disparate bits making up a whole is what we are all about."

For Luhrmann, too, the album explains why he has decided to stay working in Australia instead of heading to Hollywood, as many have urged him to do.

He grew up in a twelve-house town called Herons Creek, near Wauchope in NSW. His dad, a Vietnam veteran, bought a gas station on the highway where, Luhrmann remembers, "all these weird people came in."

When he got big enough, he found Sydney, and then the rest of the world. "But when you run out of world to question you start to look inside. You can become a great shooter for some other culture. But if you want to be a Woody Allen, a Fellini, or a Scorsese, you have to be connected to your culture. If we ever get some leadership (in Australia), I'd love to see a drive to make it attractive for creative, imaginative people to stay at home," says Luhrmann.

Talking of leadership, Luhrmann speaks admiringly of the former Prime Minister, Paul Keating. He worked on Keating's 1993 federal election campaign as a creative adviser. Luhrmann loved Keating's ideas and feels Australia has regressed, partly through the loss of them. On *Something for Everybody*, he pays tribute to the former PM with the "Jupiter Suite," which Keating chose when Luhrmann asked him which piece of music best represented Australia's self-confidence and belief in its own ideas.

Luhrmann is concerned about the current political climate here. "I think the machinery's broken. It no longer befits who we are. Until we have the self-confidence to define how to govern ourselves and, most importantly, represent ourselves to the rest of the world, we will never have the self-confidence to do anything," he says.

I ask if he can imagine a piece of music which might sum up Prime Minister John Howard's ideas. "All I can say is that, to identify a piece of music associated with him, you would have to identify a sense of spirit. I'm sure there are pieces of music he loves. But I couldn't put a piece of music to him."

He could and did, however, put music to some weird and wonderful words which came to him via the Internet. First thought to be by Kurt Vonnegut (whose name was attached to them by a prankster), "Wear Sunscreen" and other life tips to graduating students were in fact the words of *Chicago Tribune* columnist Mary Schmich. She also told her young readers to sing, floss, and not be reckless with other people's hearts.

Luhrmann thought them a great set of simple references, particularly the "Do one thing every day that scares you" one. He contacted Schmich, who was a fan of his films, negotiated the right to use her words and recorded a local actor doing the spoken element of what became "Everybody's Free (To Wear Sunscreen)."

"What I think is extraordinary, apart from the inherent values in the ideas, is that we were experiencing ourselves a historic moment in the life of the Internet, an example of how massive publishing power is in the hands of anyone with access to a PC."

Luhrmann also sees the Internet and its possibilities as being congruent with his own philosophy "to be cottage and to be in this house and part of a small team but to be able to present globally."

When Luhrmann and I spoke, the "Sunscreen" song had just been picked up by commercial radio. It was soon to be released on the college circuit in the US. He tells me people told him the *Something for Everybody* CD wouldn't work because it didn't have a singular demographic. This time he didn't heed the advice.

Luhrmann is now off to make his next film which will be shot in Australia "albeit set in Timbuktu." He says we won't hear from him for two years now until his new film is finished. "We're gone."

The Director: Baz Luhrmann

Bec Smith / 2001

From *ifMAG*, May 2001. Reprinted by permission.

"The Show Must Go On!" is the catchcry for Baz Luhrmann's latest work, *Moulin Rouge!*—and what an appropriate cry it is. While he and partner Catherine Martin have proven their knack for creative alchemy across the fields of theater, opera, and film for years now, this wildly ambitious project has been as fettered by problems as it has been fuelled by Luhrmann's legendary vision and inspiration.

"If *Romeo + Juliet* was hard," says Luhrmann, speaking down the line from the US, "this has reached new heights of challenge for me, in every regard."

Aside from personal difficulties (Baz's father died early in the shoot and lead actress Nicole Kidman cracked a rib and permanently damaged her knee), there's the project itself. Although no figures can be confirmed, the film came in well over its original budget of US$45 million and is being released six months later than originally scheduled. But this is hardly surprising given the complex nature and massive scale of the project. As Baz points out, "We knew it would be more complicated than the studio [20th Century Fox] would admit. Everything we do is like that! Every project we make, we have to say, 'Yeah, yeah, okay—if you think it can be done this way, fine.' But we always know it's going to take longer and cost more—that's just a reality. But it hasn't cost that much. It's less than your basic American comedy."

All else aside, *Moulin Rouge!* strives to be the stuff of filmmakers' dreams: innovative, a visual masterpiece, a complete reinvention of the genre. And clearly it is good enough to open the prestigious Cannes Film Festival this month. Still, Luhrmann himself admits that it's no slam dunk. "It's still very dangerous. I mean, it's still a musical, it's still opening against *Pearl Harbor*. . . ."

When we speak over the phone, Baz is still in the trenches, doing the final sound mix in LA. They're under incredible pressure: Spielberg's *AI* is closing in to take over the sound studio the day they're scheduled to finish. It's only mid-afternoon there, and Baz sounds exhausted. It's been four very intense years, even for this passionate and obsessive work-aholic. "It's a bit like you've been dropped in the ocean and you know there's an island out there if you keep swimming, and . . . it's those last few hundred meters that are most difficult."

The Vision

For over ten years, Baz Luhrmann and his key collaborator, the brilliant designer Catherine Martin (known as CM; the two are also married), have been making particular kinds of works. From their groundbreaking contemporary production of Puccini's opera *La Boheme* (1990), to their Hindi interpretation of Benjamin Britten's opera *A Midsummer Night's Dream*, to their three films (*Strictly Ballroom*, *William Shakespeare's Romeo + Juliet*, and *Moulin Rouge!*), the cornerstone of their work has always been a lavish, detailed design coupled with a barrage of postmodern cross-references. But there is more to it than a striking visual style, as Luhrmann explains.

"This belongs to a particular style we call 'red curtain' cinema. Essentially it is theatrical cinema . . . and it has some fundamental requirements: (1) the films are based on primary mythologies, so you know how they are going to end when they begin; (2) they are set in heightened creative worlds; and (3) they have some kind of device to awaken the audience's experience. They are not psychological works; they demand that the audience participate in the film."

The Myth

The primary mythology of *Moulin Rouge!* is the story of Orpheus, poet and musician, who plays such beautiful music that, when he walks by, all the trees and rocks and living things get up to follow him. When his beloved bride, Eurydice, dies on their wedding day and descends into the Underworld, Orpheus is inconsolably heartbroken—and follows her.

For thirty-eight-year-old Luhrmann, the myth is about growing up. "There is a moment in your life when you realize that things are bigger than yourself, and that—no matter who you are—you're going to have to succumb to the realities of life, or they'll destroy you."

It's hard to miss what he's referring to, on a personal level, in terms of the death of his father and the physical and emotional scars Kidman has had to endure, both with her injuries and the very public breakdown of her marriage to Tom Cruise. I ask him what his greatest joys and difficulties have been on the project, and he reflects, "Nicole and I were saying only the other day that if this story is essentially Orphean (and that myth is about learning that there are certain things that are bigger than yourself), and if, as well as that, the main gesture in the piece is 'The show must go on,' you'll see when you see the film that they are the big underlying themes, and those themes have underlined our lives. . . ."

The Process

Having established which myth to work with, Luhrmann began collaborating with his key creative team: Craig Pearce (writing), Catherine Martin (design), Anton Monsted, Marius de Vries, and Josh Abrahams (music), and Jill Bilcock (editing).

The research was exhaustive. "It wasn't just a case of saying, Okay: 1890s musical, Moulin Rouge, Orphean myth," says Luhrmann. "When I started working with Craig, for example, we looked at the whole history of bohemianism. At one stage, the film was going to be set in the seventies at Studio 54, where a young Bob Dylan type goes into an Underworld, meets Andy Warhol and the Factory and falls in love with Roller Girl at a place where there's a dance craze called disco, you know?! So you could transmutate, if you like, all the essential elements of the storytelling into other worlds. It's about finding a world that exposes and reveals that mythological story's shape."

In the end, they committed to bohemian Paris, in 1899, at a club called Moulin Rouge. . . .

A Cinematic Language

The camp sensibility, the lavish aesthetic, the overlapping pop culture references that swim across the screen before ultimately drowning one another. . . . The style Baz and CM have forged in their work is so distinctive that when Baz tells me they are considering a vast Australian pastoral work for their next picture, the only response I can manage is a stunned Wow!

But he insists that the style the world has grown to identify as theirs exists purely for this "red curtain" style of cinema. If this is the case, then how did the first two films inform *Moulin Rouge!*?

"Well, I think they're all musicals. Whichever way you look at it,

Strictly Ballroom, Romeo + Juliet, and *Moulin Rouge!* are all stories driven by rhythm and music. My initial gesture was to make *Moulin Rouge!* the finest example of red curtain cinematic work. And it's not just the movies: the 'show within the show' in *Moulin Rouge!*, for example, is a Hindi spectacular, not unlike our production of *A Midsummer Night's Dream.*"

In this way, the team builds on the success of former productions while still taking new risks. He also points out that the films refer to one other. "The 'L'Amour' sign of *La Boheme* and the 'Coke' sign of *Strictly Ballroom* and the 'Coke L'Amour' of *Romeo + Juliet* have reappeared as the 'L'Amour Fou Lingerie' sign in *Moulin Rouge!*" But why cross-reference such signs and symbols? "It's a particular way of telling. Not everyone loves it, but it's our way of telling stories. And," he says emphatically, "I intend to move on."

Roots

Although the Luhrmann bus travels all over the world (*Romeo + Juliet* was shot on location in Mexico, cut in Australia, and finished in America), *Moulin Rouge!* saw the entire team at Sydney's Fox Studios, where recently constructed large sound stages made it possible for them to complete this huge project on home turf.

A mansion in Darlinghurst called "Iona" served as home and creative base for Baz during the project. That its imposing, twisted gothic iron gates adjoin the falling wooden pails of *ifMAG*'s feels like a metaphor for the still uneasy co-existence of big international projects and small independent ones on the Australian film landscape, a topic Baz clearly has strong views on.

"We invested all of our money in setting up our company in Australia because we believe we have to live in, and work from, Australia—with Australian partners—as much as we possibly can. Ninety-five percent of the team was Australian." Why? "Because it's our language. We have a very specific way of telling stories, and we can maintain that because we stay connected to our roots and who we are. This is not a judgement of people who have become shooters in other cultures, but we are Australians. That's the answer. I mean, why is it important to work in Australia? Because we're Australians, that's why!"

Last November, despite flying out to LA the following day, Luhrmann took time out to speak at *ifMAG*'s awards ceremony. On the night, he said he believed that, for the first time, Australia was in a situation where it could realistically host big budget productions that would ultimately feed into the independent sector. How does he feel now that his project is coming to a close?

"I don't know is the answer," he says, "because we've got to bring it out and see what happens. I think there'll be a lot of positive and negative dialogue about it. It'll be like, 'Well that's all right for him, but what about us?' [But] what I said at the *if* awards still stands, which is that, no matter which way you look at it, opportunity is still in our laps." He believes it is the collective responsibility of everyone in the Australian film industry to ensure that large scale production feeds back into the independent sector. "It behoves 20th Century Fox and it behoves the government to make sure that they are sinking money back into [Australia] and planting the seeds. You know, today's independent filmmaker is tomorrow's Tarantino or Spielberg or Jane Campion," he says.

"Where we are very different from the American system is that we have the chance to build our industry and guide it in the way in which we'd like to see it evolve—if we maintain that power. And that's a very, very important issue. I think it's too easy to hide in a frightened corner and say, 'Oh my God, you know, we can't do anything about it. We're being invaded!' I think that's a bit sad, you know?"

The Rub

One contentious issue circulating on the ground in Sydney during the production of *Moulin Rouge!* was that, on a film with a budget of US$45 million, actors were paid minimum Equity rates.

"Well, let me say something," says Luhrmann. "Nicole Kidman was paid Equity rates, and Ewan McGregor. Myself, I gave all my money to the film. Now, that's not to laud that, but I could not have made this film if I, or anybody else, pulled their first full wage. So I said, 'Look, here are the rules. They're not the rules for everybody, but this is how we're going to make the film.'

"And," he continues, "I mean, for Nicole or Ewan to work on this film, they had to give up two or three other multi-million-dollar-earning incomes. So they should be more part of the pie more than, say, someone who is doing their first film.

"Mostly people spend their time going, 'I wish I was working on something I found creatively exciting or challenging.' I mean, Richard Roxburgh sings in this movie. He gets to sing, you know? You can't make a musical, get to sing, and do things that you're not normally cast to do, and expect to get paid your top dollar. If I was making a film that was basically exploiting people's already identified market worth, that's different. But no one in this film is known for being a romantic song and dance person. They're all breaking new markets.

"I think people who say that really have no concept whatsoever of how market worth works globally," says Luhrmann. "I mean, an actor, right? Their market worth is based purely on how many people they'll attract to the cinema. And we don't actually have anybody in this film who's considered a film opener—and I mean all our stars inclusive."

At this point I can hear the exasperation in his voice, bordering on an almost manic hilarity. "You know how much this film should have cost to make is easily $100 million! And simply no one would give me that amount of money."

Raise the Curtain

So given the riskiness of the project and all that he and others have put into it, how is Baz feeling now that it's about to open Cannes?

"Well, there's just a lot of work to do—and one is never sure. All I can say is that the first independent people to actually see it were the two selectors at Cannes, and obviously they've got some confidence. But I'm only ever about 50 percent happy with anything I do, so we'll see. . . ."

On with the show!

Moulin Rouge!

Serena Donadoni / 2001

From *The Cinema Girl* (blog), 2001, thecinemagirl.com. Reprinted by permission of the author.

"People want to see music and story work together," says filmmaker Baz Luhrmann, "and I think we've got the cinematic language. Music unites us. It transcends time and geography and unites us no matter what our backgrounds. Definitely, music has a power beyond our literal understanding. Now if you can collude that with the act of storytelling, it is a powerful and unstoppable force."

The genesis of Luhrmann's latest spectacle, the glorious postmodern musical *Moulin Rouge!* (2001), came from a visit to the Parisian nightclub whose infamous can-can is now merely canned entertainment for tourists anxious to glimpse bohemian naughtiness. He may have gone there for kitsch (LaToya Jackson's snake act), but Luhrmann found enough echoes of the Moulin Rouge's avant-garde era—phantasmagoric fin de siècle decadence captured by painter Henri de Toulouse-Lautrec—that it sparked something in his feverish imagination.

"I just had this realization," Luhrmann says in Los Angeles, "that here was a lot of the beginnings of popular culture as we know it today: Debussy, Ravel, and Satie equal pop music, Toulouse-Lautrec, Andy Warhol and the Factory. The whole idea of where we are today started to come from this extraordinary time and place. So I had the desire to recapture that spirit."

Since he has a hand in every detail of his extraordinarily textured films (*Strictly Ballroom, William Shakespeare's Romeo + Juliet*), it's hardly a surprise to learn that Luhrmann's favorite part of making movies comes before the cameras ever start rolling. "I love the research," he enthuses, "I love the getting into the life of the film, getting into the characters, understanding their world, becoming completely and utterly absorbed with the world of the film."

The idea he brought back to the Sydney-based creative team he heads with wife and collaborator Catherine Martin was a story set in 1899 Paris which would blend classical elements (the Orpheus myth) and nineteenth-century popular tales (*Camille*, *La Boheme*, and Emile Zola's *Nana*) with an end of the millennium sensibility. With *Moulin Rouge!*, Luhrmann would infuse the movie musical with elements of opera and give it a new spin by filling the soundtrack with reinterpretations of contemporary pop songs. (The exception is "Come What May," specifically written by David Baerwald for the film.)

"Baz kept talking about it," recalls Martin, who is *Moulin Rouge!*'s production and costume designer, "in terms of real artificiality as opposed to artificial reality. So that was kind of the philosophy that we had. Then, of course, we took the sort of nineteenth-century baroqueness and gave it a bit of a tweak."

Growing up in the tiny hamlet of Herons Creek in Australia, Luhrmann fell in love with the Hollywood musicals shown in the cinema his father ran along with the family farm and gas station. He was attracted to the way musicals could set their own rules and create remarkable, insular worlds where reality was heightened. (Luhrmann adopted this philosophy and that, along with the bold aesthetic he created with Martin, marked the future filmmaker as the enfant terrible of Australian theater.)

"It's the nature of musicals," he explains, "that they are decadent and lush and you get a sense that everything is extreme. However, one engages in degrees of discipline in it. The intensity of it—the muchness, if you like—is actually inherent in traditional musical language."

While researching a stage musical, Luhrmann travelled to India and was captivated by a Hindi-language Bollywood film, whose hedonistic splendour and grand gestures also engendered the audience's emotional devotion. It would serve as a model for *Moulin Rouge!*

"The one thing I haven't heard anyone say about the movie is that it's boring," says Nicole Kidman, whose consumptive courtesan Satine falls for Ewan McGregor's Christian, an impoverished writer. "It is amazing," she continues, "how you can depict strong emotions like jealousy or love or obsession through music and dance far more readily [than through straightforward dialogue]. Once we embraced that concept during the love scenes—being able to sing "Come What May" to each other, or instead of whispering in each other's ear, actually singing—it made it easier in a strange way."

A sequence where Kidman and McGregor sing atop a sixty-foot gilded elephant (a structure modelled on an actual Moulin Rouge annex which served as an opium den) defines their relationship via a song ingeniously constructed from bits of pop nuggets as diverse as U2's "Pride (In the Name of Love)," Paul McCartney's "Silly Love Songs," Dolly Parton's "I Will Always Love You," and the Kiss staple," I Was Made for Loving You."

"In the *Elephant Love Medley*," says Catherine Martin, "you really get that thing of people speaking through song. This is a fabulously joyous musical conversation and you can really see the investment of the actors in that scene because that's what carries it: that they actually act through the song." "That was what Baz wanted," concurs Nicole Kidman, "to keep the plot and the love story and the emotions that were being depicted present and alive during those scenes."

Luhrmann's belief in the power of music—his oddball single "Everybody's Free (To Wear Sunscreen)" was an international hit—is behind this $50 million experiment, one which may revive a moribund genre. It isn't the first or last chance he'll take in a diverse career driven by the radically simple desire to continually make life more interesting.

"We're off-the-road people," he explains, "and what I mean by that is: once you get on a specific track, it's very hard to get off it. What actually defines bohemia, in a sense, is the ability to wake up in the morning and say, 'You know what? We're not going that way anymore.' That you're in control of where you're travelling to and how you're travelling."

"The freedom to go where you want," he adds, "that's the upside. The payment is the risk inherent in that."

Millennial Mambo:
Baz Luhrmann Messes with the Musical
Because He Can-Can

Ray Pride / 2001

A shorter version of this interview was originally published in *Expresso* (Lisboa), June 2001. This version is reprinted by the author's permission.

Australian director Baz Luhrmann wants to astonish. He says he wants to "reinvent musical cinema," and, in his first two movies, *Strictly Ballroom* and *William Shakespeare's Romeo + Juliet*, he took his first tentative steps, making a frenetic scratch-mix of music and history with all the prankish savvy of contemporary theater and opera directors.

Contemporary American movies are usually slaves to naturalism, but with his third film, *Moulin Rouge!*, Luhrmann is a slave only to the rhythm. Making a movie that is choking with extravagance and detail and a love of "love," Luhrmann is working in a form akin to Paul Thomas Anderson's *Magnolia*: an impatient, operatic too-muchness. He designs and directs and music-produces not as though he'd never be allowed to make a movie again, but as if no movie would ever be made again.

While the story is a mass hallucination of the half-remembered tropes of the turn-of-the-century Parisian bohemian epoch, the music draws from dozens of sources with improvident alacrity. Luhrmann's show-within-the-show is an India-set stage production that mimics the wild fantasias of multi-hour Bollywood musical epics, and the feast is for the eyes as well as the ears. But the ditty-simple libretto simply sets us in Montmartre, 1899, where "a Bohemian storm is brewing."

Courtesan Satine (Nicole Kidman, icy, then champagne-giggly) finds her future and that of the Moulin Rouge nightclub have been staked by lascivious impresario Zidler (Jim Broadbent, bellowingly merry) on her accommodation of a dweeby Duke (Richard Roxburgh). Young writer

Christian (Ewan McGregor), new to the quartier, falls in with Toulouse-Lautrec (John Leguizamo, playing him as the truth-telling soul of the scene), who leads a bohemian band of artists who are impressed only with "truth, beauty, freedom, and love." Lautrec pushes Christian and Satine into each other's arms in a screwball comedy turn of mistaken identity: Satine believes Christian is the Duke. Cue the recurring refrain: "The greatest thing you'll ever learn is just to love and be loved in return."

An absinthe-drenched reimagining of pop opera and the American musical comedy, each and every scene is a full-throated shouting down of any notion of understatement. Luhrmann is fixed on attaining the authentic through the inauthentic. How do we get to genuine feeling when we've been told how to feel so many times in movies and songs?

Contemporary American movies are feats of naturalism, but with *Moulin Rouge!*, Luhrmann and co. are interested in feats of levitation. They're willing to tempt the notion: Can you die of too much beauty? If anything will sell the movie to the world at large, it's the dense, generous, postmodern soundtrack, delineating the recombinant DNA of a century of pop music: the "cancan" heard in *Moulin Rouge!* is courtesy of Norman Cook (Fatboy Slim) who sings, "Because you can-can-can!" over a track in his family rave-cum-frat-party fashion.

The movie unfurls on vast, lavish sets filled with color and action, augmented with swooping, physically impossible, computer-effects-enhanced shots of the end-of-the-century capital by day and night. The Duke agrees to finance a show, which mirrors the love-intrigues in the "real" world and is designed and told in the excessive, brilliantly colored style of Bollywood musical epics. But you don't have to know that for the movie's look and insurgent soundtrack to knock your socks off. Everything is iconic: the characters exist only in our visual rapture (or lack thereof) in watching them maneuver around their feelings through song.

Most effective is how Luhrmann and co. weave their soundtrack from dozens of sources, with the actors singing their own roles (Kidman's is lovely but thin; McGregor's is pretty damn terrific). The best example might be a love duet between Satine and Christian, when they are in full swoon over one another, which starts with bits of Phil Collins' "One More Night," segues into U2's "Pride: In the Name of Love," veers into "Don't Leave Me This Way," Paul McCartney's "Silly Love Songs," "Up Where We Belong," and then David Bowie and Brian Eno's soaring dirge to teenage love, "Heroes." The ace in the hole? The medley then moves to the climactic soar of Dolly Parton's "I Will Always Love You" and Elton John's "Your Song." Sounds either dizzying or dumb, but, in fact, it soars above jokiness into some kind of sensation that finds emotional authenticity in the most synthetic parts of our shared pop consciousness.

The "we" that Luhrmann compulsively alludes to in conversation is less royal than communal, encompassing several key Bazmark Inq. collaborators, including production and costume designer Catherine Martin ("CM"), to whom he is married, and Craig Pearce, his co-writer. Feline and impatient, Luhrmann is a cat who is self-consciously hep. With a shoulder-length fall of nicotine-to-gray hair, the 38-year-old impresario loves "a bit of a chat." Luhrmann is one of the fastest talkers I've ever encountered, and is willing to let his thoughts tumble over each other in his clipped, sometimes nasal speech, as this slightly edited transcript demonstrates. (While there are discussions of plot turns in the conversation that follows, the same information is also provided in the opening moments of narration.) These conversations took place at the Raffles L'Ermitage Hotel in Beverly Hills on May 13 and 14, 2001, a few days after the Cannes 2001 opening night debut of *Moulin Rouge!*

Ray Pride: The refrain from "Heroes" in the big production number is bugging me right now.
Baz Luhrmann: [pleased] Is it?

RP: That and the da-DAH-da-DAH of the "Because you can-can-can" refrain.
BL: I think the fun thing about it is taking a song you've lived with for many, many years. The device in that duet is that it's all pop, and we're dealing with it in a very classical form. Because it's emotional storytelling, it does stick, you know what I mean? Like opera. In terms of what I like on my turntable, I would love to have heard Beck do a remix of it or something.

RP: That song's meant something to me since I was nineteen, and I'm bringing the back-story of the lyrics to the scene, of Bowie in a hotel room watching a pair of teenage lovers on either side of barbed wire between East and West Berlin, at risk of being shot if they make contact.
BL: Yeah.

RP: And you make it so exuberant, soaring, when Satine and Christian light up toward each other in the medley.

BL: It's inherent. I think what you pick up there proves to me that when a piece of art is true, it transcends time and geography. Let's take your point on "Heroes." Whether you knew that story or not, (the link you make with the original clip) is embodied in that: it's a hero's song, about a boy and girl saying, "Look, just for one day. . . ." It's got incredible hope yet sadness in it. Then when, suddenly, it's transplanted to a scene that has the same notion embodied in it, it amplifies the emotion. Same with, say, the tango piece, right?

RP: There's a Flaubert quotation I ran across the other day that seems to suit our give-and-take about process: "Talent is long patience, and originality an effort of will and intense observation."
BL: Boy, has he been around recently in my gig? I don't know if I'm very talented, but I do know that creativity is exactly as he says. There is this perception that someone who makes something goes up on a mountain and simply imagines it. The process so often gets mystified like that. But it's one thing to have an idea and another thing to make it actually happen.

RP: I admire at least the simple description of your communal process, a kind of magpie distillation of all these influences. It's like a rare, modest idea that a "vision" can work this way, that it doesn't burst fully-formed from one ego.
BL: It can't. Unless you're a painter and it is a relationship between you and the canvas, then the moment you step outside that situation and involve one other person, what you get is totally a collaboration. My job is to know where we are heading. How we get there is totally in the hands of many.

I've only ever known that process, from working with my brothers as a kid to what I'm doing now. It's a richer, better experience to work with people. I think that probably what I contribute to the process is that I help others to give forth.

RP: I was talking to CM yesterday about the idea of "raising the temperature of the room," the idea that the challenges people who respect and know each other can throw each other make the work smarter and richer and better.
BL: Totally. What we do is argue. [laughs] But in a really right way. What I mean by that is that it's not personal, it's just dut-dut-a-dutta-dut and it's fun. We are addicted to it.

RP: From the interviews you did for *Romeo + Juliet* and from the pre-release interviews for *Moulin Rouge!*, the most common set of words you use is "I believe in love." I was wondering how, for you, *Moulin Rouge!* is the culmination of your three films about the killing and thrilling aspects of love?

BL: Well, that's a good one, that's a good one. [Luhrmann stands, to illustrate the idea while pacing, folding his jacket over a chair.] *Strictly Ballroom* is like the pure white light that's triumphantly perfect at the end: y'know, they live happily ever after . . . well, they get together. It has the resonance of, y'know, love triumphs over oppression, right? We all know that. Boy and girl, young, we will not be artistically oppressed, let's fight side by side, we fall in love, we triumph. But what happens after that? What's the sequel? One doesn't deal with that in a kind of David and Goliath myth, y'know. We don't go and see Scott and Fran move on, move out to the suburbs, open a dance school and argue, and he has an affair. Don't want to deal with that. That's the purity of that myth.

Romeo + Juliet is about love in conflict with society: it's tragic, it's purely the other way. *Strictly Ballroom* is purely positive, this is purely negative. We completely lose that (in *Moulin Rouge!*). It's more about what happens to the adult world instead of what happens to them. Satine discovers love before she dies. She is "like a virgin, touched for the very first time."

RP: Touched by love for the very first time.

BL: The first time. Because Satine is born to a world of prostitution. And if you know someone born to the world of prostitution, you don't ask them, "Why are you a prostitute?" The answer is too simple. It's like, there's that, then there's eating. So she's never been able to be emotionally involved. She discovers that just before she dies. Christian has this absolute ideal that love will conquer all. But then he discovers that, actually, it won't, that he can't control things. His jealousy makes him do a dumb thing and he almost loses her. But right at the very end, y'know, the curtain comes down on them. Whereas love triumphs at the end of *Strictly Ballroom*, what Satine and Christian both discover is something bigger than love, and that's death. Something they can't control.

Death steals away Satine. But just before they part, what they discover is the point of the film. For Satine, it's better to have loved and lost than never to have loved at all. And it's the same for Christian, one hopes, although he has lost this naive, idealistic perception of love, y'know, pure, absolute, unswerving. He's scared, but he goes on, changed. He doesn't give up on it altogether.

I basically believe that your relationship to love evolves. I don't only believe it, I've experienced it. I've been Mr. Young-I-Will-Never-You-Will-Never-We-Will-Always. We've all done that.

RP: Got older and done that. The youthful tack can be delirious, even ridiculous, but you can remember it to find the necessary level now. . . .
BL: That's right. That's right. You realize that, actually, there's another kind of love, y'know. I suppose the bottom line is this: this is an easy answer, or a short one anyway. There's got to be something good about growing old. You've gotta get something in place of all the apparent magnificence of youth that disappears as the years go by, the diamonds of youth and beauty that disappear as you move through life. And that's a kind of spirituality, a bigger spiritual power.

RP: It's also the role someone finds themselves playing toward love, as you grow older. A woman I know who's just turned thirty finally decided to have someone live with her. Now she's horrified, constantly irritated. I said, "I guess you don't want to be the old couple sitting around." Actually, she does, but with the wrong person, it's turning her manic.
BL: That's right. You've hit the magic number: thirty. This is a generalization, but you turn thirty and that little bit of thing called youth, which you're not aware of when you're young, is going. As Orson Welles said [does jokey Welles voice], "I know what it's like to be young, but you don't know what it's like to be old." It's quite true. You don't realize when you're under thirty what a get-out-of-jail-free card you've got. Y'know? Then slam, down comes the cage at thirty.

There's a reason why Hamlet is that age. Romeo has one characteristic: absolutism. Hamlet is the complete opposite: he can't make up his mind about anything. Macbeth, having gone through that arc, is now engorged with power, and Lear is a silly old man, in a sense. They all have the kind of primary fault of their age.

RP: Speaking of Shakespeare, that brings up an interesting trend among some of the more interesting filmmakers working today, after they've made a few films: the willingness to be simple and direct. Audiences don't seem to have a problem accepting things being direct once they're in the seats, but, sadly, with recent work from filmmakers like Wong Kar Wai, von Trier, Wayne Wang, there doesn't seem to be a critical vocabulary to discuss simple emotionality. That's going to be a problem with the way *Moulin Rouge!* gets described as well. Simplicity and directness are sometimes taken for sentimentality or simple-mindedness.

BL: Look, it's really simple. I've made this kind of work all my life. I don't need to justify it. I spent the first fifteen years of my working creative life doing Brecht and Artaud, materials that were so complex my mother couldn't understand what they were.

Exactly the same critical response was levelled at Shakespeare and Molière. Because what they were dealing with were audiences from children to the Queen of England. What they had to find was a simplicity in story structure, but a resonance and complexity in the layering. It's kind of naive not to understand the difference between those things.

One's got to be really, really committed to the journey, the journey of making the art to be received by the audience. It's not a demographic I'm chasing, it's a psychographic. Otherwise you withdraw and all you're doing is hiding in the kind of "let's hold up signs and symbols that tell a lot of critical folk that they can feel comfortable." And it's easy to get drawn into that.

RP: So would a label like "delirious kitsch" be a problem for you?

BL: Well, what are we talking about here? Tastefulness? Because what is kitsch? If we were talking about classical Greek art, statues, and the wall of the Acropolis, we might think of that as being profoundly "tasteful." But it was painted in disco colors in the time of the Greeks. I mean, all of those statues had rouge and pink faces and brightly colored clothes.

RP: Color was expensive. Only the rich could afford to be gaudy. Only they had perfume and finery.

BL: That's right. It's a funny thing about kitsch. If you're going to make a screwball comedy, for example, why can't you make it look like an MGM musical? Whenever I've ever had someone in the ring about this, they kind of disappear into zero. I remember, in Spain, one guy went into a mumbling thing about "Well, y'know, I just know it's wrong." And I said, well, I made a film where there was an all-powerful federation, the president going, "There's only one way to cha-cha-cha, mate, and you're breaking the rule book." When you put rules, so-called invisible rules, next to art, you know someone's insecure about something.

RP: Sometimes we don't want to admit we're swept away by a movie, so this kind of complaint is a way of resisting that engagement.

BL: What you're pinpointing is important. It's all about "audience participation cinema": it demands of you that you participate. It says to an audience, "Hey, whoa-whoa, wake up, wake up, you've gotta be involved or forget it, get out, y'know. If you're not gonna get on the bus, you won't get anything at the end." It's not a state that people who go in to do their critiques are necessarily ready for. It's not a criticism of the critique people [laughs]. But in all honesty, if you're not ready to be manipulated, there's no point. Y'know, ask for your money back.

RP: *Moulin Rouge!* is bold even from frame one: the big red curtain even before the Fox logo, and then the tiny conductor leading the orchestra as the curtains part and we see the logo. . . .
BL: And from moment one, you're being let in on the deal. You're being told that we're going to manipulate you.

RP: You have to bring something of yourself to observing any art. And sometimes we reveal more about ourselves through what we react against than what we claim to love.
BL: I've only got one concern. It's not the war between the 50 percent who defend what I do and the 50 percent who attack it. It's that the people that need *Strictly Ballroom*, or who need *Romeo + Juliet*, or who need this film, are caught in the crossfire. I'm not saying, like, we're here to save the world, but there are audiences that need theatricality rather than naturalism to be touched and feel. I don't want them to get caught in the crossfire. And it's not like the viewpoints are fixed from the time films are released. The rewriting of the history on *Romeo + Juliet* is quite staggering.

RP: *Salon*'s review from when *Romeo + Juliet* was released calls it "garish junk" and goes on to say, "It takes a special kind of idiot to screw up *Romeo and Juliet*, but then Baz Luhrmann isn't your garden variety idiot."
BL: The great thing about that is that it is so staggeringly humiliating for that critic. If you live by the critique game, you die by the critique game. On the other hand, a very famous American critic came to me and apologized for his review of *Romeo + Juliet*. In a film class he'd been teaching, he had screened it and a different view of it emerged.

RP: Maybe it's naturalism rather than theatricality that's the unnatural state.

BL: Just show me a musical where you've had naturalism in the plot structure. There is a reason why we reference very directly Emile Zola's *Nana* and *Lady of the Camellias* and *La Bohème* in *Moulin Rouge!* They are all drawing on the same, recognizable, well-worn story structure.

It's not that you expect people to go, "Aha! A beat out of *Nana*." I expect them to recognize a story about a middle-class boy meeting a prostitute who's dying of consumption and that what follows is going to be a tragic story. Shorthanding gives us poetic resonance and that's valuable, y'know. That's what's really important.

RP: There's the bromide that clichés persist for a reason.

BL: Well, cliché and myth are basically a picture of our condition, and they allow truths to appear.

RP: Let's talk about something even more obvious. You like to re-purpose popular song.

BL: In terms of trying to create a musical language that works now, there are two points to make. One is that it's quite an old idea. When Judy Garland sings "Clang-clang-clang went the trolley" in *Meet Me in St. Louis*, the period is 1900 and she's singing 1943 music off the radio. This helped the audiences of the time to get inside the character and the story, to understand a different time and place through their own music. The second thing is that it's a basic rule of musicals, that the audience have a pre-existing relationship with the music. "White Christmas," for example, is sung in two or three films, at least.

RP: Were the rights issues tough?

BL: I had to meet with publishing companies. They think, "My God, this is a new way to use our catalogue music. This could be good!" Some of the people who wrote the music we used are friends of mine, like Bono, y'know? He's a good pal. Others, like Bowie and Elton, I just had to meet with them and go through what I was doing and they all loved the idea. "My song being used in a musical? Now that would be good." Because these people would be writing musicals if we were in the 1940s now. They were very, very positive.

RP: Any you couldn't get?

BL: Yes. Cat Stevens's "Father and Son." It was sad, because it was a great scene. At the beginning of the film, we wanted Christian's dad to go (growling the lyrics), "It's not time to make a change, just relaxxxx. . . ."

RP: Did you approach him?

BL: No. In fact, he's almost impossible to meet with. We dialogued with his brother and, look, I respect why he rejected it. It was on religious grounds, because Christian and Satine are not married. So it's really simple. I completely understood that, but he was the only one.

RP: Rodgers and Hammerstein let you have a lot of play with *The Sound of Music*.

BL: They were fantastic. In fact, they have been historically like that. They've got this really groovy, swinging board and they're really, like, "Yeah! How can we get this music into a more interesting and modern context?" In an early script, there was a moment where Toulouse says (Luhrmann adopting the character's thick-tongued lisp), "Lotth of healthy Bohemian outdoor thex! Rolling in the thnow!" He was describing the show to the Duke, and Rodgers and Hammerstein's board wrote back that they really liked this idea and that they particularly liked the "lots of Bohemian outdoor sex" line. Which, unfortunately, I had to cut. . . . So, y'know. . . .

RP: In a way, *Moulin Rouge!* is one long, unrelenting set piece. Artifice, unrelenting. So what about Toulouse's line, when he spits out at the Duke, the financier of *Spectacular Spectacular*, "I am against your stupid dogma!"?

Luhrmann: Yeahhhh. . . . That came up when we were in Cannes. An army of people came up and said, "We got your wink about Dogme." But in truth, really, we didn't. Lars and all those guys, y'know, we're all distant cousins. We've watched each other's work for a long time and Bazmark has its own dogma.

RP: So your Dogme is your line about Red Curtain Cinema?

BL: Red Curtain Cinema, yes. It is audience participation cinema. It is a cinema that demands of the audience that they participate. It is theatricalized cinema. It tells very common stories where you know how it's going to end from the time it begins. It utilizes devices to wake you up: music, iambic pentameter, whatever. You're involved. That's the philosophy.

RP: But you're not espousing it for anyone else?

BL: No, no. And I don't think the Dogme guys are that serious about it.

They're not saying, "All films should be like that." It's kind of like a club with a particular way of thinking.

I'm sure there are people who might think that I must be a zealot. But my view is: you have a story, you have a notion to convey it, you invent a cinematic language for it. *Moulin Rouge!* is the last Red Curtain film I'll be doing. The next piece will have a completely different cinematic language. When you start believing that "there's only one way to cha-cha-cha," you're in trouble. When you start listening to people who tell you that there's a rulebook about art, you've got a problem. You must have your own way of telling your stories. When David Hockney, who's a great fan of our operas, talks about painting, he says, "It's my way of seeing." We always have to find our way of telling.

RP: What killed the musical?

BL: Action is king right now. Right? There was a time when musicals were king, and when sword-and-sandal was king. Then we hit a period, the 1970s, and it was all about extreme reality, *Mean Streets*, y'know, reality cinema. It was about filmmakers destroying the artifice of their parents. I mean, Martin Scorsese's parents were into musicals. The circle just goes round. Stories don't change, just how you tell them. And what we are doing, I think is a kind of reaction against super-naturalism.

The Man behind the Red Curtain

Terry Keefe / 2001

From Hollywood Interview (www.theHollywoodInterview.com) and *Venice Magazine*, June 2001. Reprinted by permission of the author.

The "Red Curtain" is a descriptive phrase coined by filmmaker Baz Luhrmann to describe his style of filmmaking, and it is apt. His is a cinema which is so highly theatrical that it feels like it was birthed from the stage. Think of the fevered final dance competition of his debut feature, *Strictly Ballroom* (1992), which was so colorful and high-octane that it almost seemed to be an animated film come to life. Or the swirling camera and dazzling production design which breathed new life into the oft-told story of *Romeo + Juliet* (1996). Luhrmann's films take place in a world that can best be described as heightened reality, and they combine elements of theater, opera, traditional cinema, and numerous elements of pop culture to create an almost completely new genre. The universe behind Luhrmann's red curtain is always on ten, and it demands that the audience be anything but passive. In a Luhrmann film, you know you're watching a movie, but it sometimes feels more like a live performance. So much, in fact, that audiences at the Cannes Film Festival this year were applauding at the end of each of the songs in Luhrmann's newest feature film, *Moulin Rouge!*, as if they were at a Broadway show.

Moulin Rouge! takes place at the turn of twentieth-century Paris and tells the story of a young musical playwright, Christian (Ewan McGregor), who falls in love with Satine (Nicole Kidman), the star of the decadently infamous Moulin Rouge nightclub. Satine also happens to be the city's most famous courtesan, and this is where trouble enters paradise. Zidler (Jim Broadbent), the Moulin Rouge's P. T. Barnum–like impresario, has promised the hand of Satine to the Duke of Worchester (a delightfully evil Richard Roxburgh). In exchange, the Duke will finance a renovation of the Moulin Rouge into a legitimate theater, where Satine can become a true actress. It's a tale of love vs. money. Did we mention that it's also a musical? A musical in which McGregor and Kidman sing everything from the title track of *The Sound of Music* to David Bowie's "Heroes."

With *Moulin Rouge!*, Luhrmann reinvents the movie musical by delving into the past. It's almost as if he took all the music videos, studio musicals, pop albums, and stage productions of the last hundred years, stuck them into a Cuisinart, and proceeded to shape *Moulin Rouge!* out of the mixture. There are so many pop culture references in *Moulin Rouge!* that there are references within the references: such as the scene in which Nicole Kidman croons Madonna's *Material Girl* as a bunch of tuxedoed male suitors chase her around with gifts, while the imagery references the 1985 video for the Madonna song. But wait, that video was itself an homage to the scene in the film *Gentlemen Prefer Blondes* (1953) in which Marilyn Monroe sings "Diamonds Are a Girl's Best Friend," which, incidentally, Kidman also sings here. *Moulin Rouge!* showcases the Red Curtain style at its most full-blown yet. It even opens with a shot of a red curtain which pulls back to reveal one of the most dazzling opening sequences in recent cinematic memory, as Luhrmann's camera flies over a recreation of the cityscape of Paris, zips into various apartments to introduce some of the lead characters, then rockets into the Moulin Rouge nightclub for the opening number.

The roots of Luhrmann's groundbreaking cinema can be traced back to his extensive theatrical background in his home country of Australia. While studying to be an actor at Sydney's National Institute of Dramatic Art, Luhrmann co-wrote, staged, and directed a play which he would develop into his film, *Strictly Ballroom*. But before he made the jump to film, Luhrmann would produce his first opera, *Lake Lost*, which is where he began his long collaboration with his wife and production designer, Catherine Martin. During subsequent opera productions of *La Boheme* and *A Midsummer Night's Dream*, Luhrmann and Martin would develop their signature style which would eventually be brought to the world of cinema.

We caught up with him on the eve of the nationwide opening of *Moulin Rouge!*, which had already completed a highly successful limited release in New York and Los Angeles. In both cities, audiences were lining up around the block to get a glimpse of what's behind the red curtain.

Terry Keefe: When you were at the conceptual stages of *Moulin Rouge!*, did you know that you'd basically be re-inventing the movie musical by the time you were done?

Baz Luhrmann: Yes, that was what we set out to do. Apart from the other things that feed the process of deciding what to make, it's always been a desire of mine. I grew up in the middle of nowhere and we got lots of old television shows and my dad ran a cinema for a while, so I loved musicals as a kid. You know, all this artificiality making you feel things. I've done a lot of opera and theater, and I just thought that somebody's got to get around to making that work in the cinema again. So that was the project.

TK: With all the songs, dance, and production design you had to try out, this couldn't have been a traditional scripting process.
BL: You know, this is the third of this kind of film that we've done. We set out to make a cinematic form which is the antithesis of the current cinema vernacular. Where the audience participate. Where they are awakened. Where they are alive in the cinema. Where they are actually uniting with the rest of the people in the cinema and participating.

Now, the film's played in both New York and Los Angeles, in just two cinemas, but the audiences are clapping in exactly the same places. And that's good news for us, because it's what makes the film different. I mention this because we built *Strictly Ballroom*, *Romeo + Juliet*, and this film in the same manner. Our methods are very labor-intensive. We spend a lot of time doing very detailed academic research. Then we build the plot-line and, believe me, it's very difficult to build a simple plot. All the films tell simple, recognizable stories whose ending the audience knows when it begins. And when people know the plot, it's all about the execution.

TK: A lot of the rehearsal for *Moulin Rouge!* occurred at a place of yours in Australia called "The House of Iona," described in the production notes as a "sprawling Victorian mansion." Tell us about that.
BL: It's a production facility, but we also live there. The key actors came there for four weeks. The same thing happened on *Romeo + Juliet*: Leonardo DiCaprio came and lived with us for a while as we developed it. We take working with the actors very seriously: they do their work and then we redraft based on what happens in the rehearsals and the workshopping.

TK: What was the casting process for the leads like? Was it always a requirement that they could sing, or did you ever consider casting non-singing stars that you could dub?

BL: They had to be able to sing. And I know of many, many famous actors who can sing beautifully. I had had some contact with both Ewan and Nicole before. I did a photo shoot with Nicole for *Vogue*—I was the editor for an issue—and I knew she was very funny and warm and unlike the Nicole that most people know about. And I almost cast Ewan as Mercutio (in *Romeo + Juliet*).

I went through the process of finding out what actors could fulfil the roles and then convey emotion through voice. They didn't have to be big singers, but they had to be able to move you emotionally. They had to be able to act through voice. Basically, Ewan and Nicole were the best for the job. That was the bottom line.

TK: Is it true you weren't able to screen-test Ewan and Nicole together before making the final casting decision?

BL: Yes, Nicole was on stage on Broadway in *The Blue Room* and Ewan was in the West End in a play as well. So I really had to take a punt on that chemistry and, I must say, Ronna Kress, my casting director, really held my hand and said, "Look, you've got to take the leap of faith." We did and there really was a chemical reaction between the two of them.

TK: How was the on-camera singing filmed?

BL: We used all the techniques. There's the traditional technique of playback, which is your basic one: they record and we do playback on the set. But we also used a groundbreaking technique which is where they sing live and then you replace the voice later with digital technology. It's a program which locks what you've sung to lip-sync. And alongside that, for a few moments in the film, they're actually singing live.

TK: I have to ask you how you created the fantastic opening where you're zipping in and out of all those buildings and all over the city of Paris.

BL: It's a combination of very old techniques and very new techniques. The illusion that it's black and white film and then we zoom in: that is all model work, old-fashioned models. Then we used digital technology to put in boats and water and sky and people. We shot hundreds of little extras. There are tiny little people walking on the bridge and things to make it look real.

So it's a combination of old and new. We spent all of our digital money, and we didn't have a lot of it, making things not good but bad. Basically stopping it from looking digitally perfect, making it look "cinematically imperfect."

TK: What types of techniques were used to make it look imperfect?

BL: You can equate this with the difference between digital sound and analog. They're like CDs vs. vinyl records. Life in digital is absolutely mathematically perfect. Unfortunately, real life is nothing like that. In fact, it's the imperfections between individual violin strings that make an orchestra warm. They're all slightly out of tune. That's why, when you get a digital sample of a violin and you put hundreds of them together, they sound nothing like the real thing. Because it's the imperfection that makes something warm. And we've done that a lot on *Moulin Rouge!*

For example, when we have our camera sweeping through buildings over Paris in the opening, we had to actually digitally program-in the imperfections of bumps and shakes. At first, you really do believe you might be watching a bit of black and white footage, and that's because it shakes. Also, if you look at the shot, it goes out of focus. We had to digitally put it out of focus.

TK: What are some of your favorite movie musicals?

BL: I think that I have tastes that range from *Top Hat* to *The Band Wagon* to *Cabaret*. I love the early Elvis musicals, but I also love *West Side Story*, which is a tragedy.

TK: You're willing to take a lot of risks that most directors would never hang their career on. Can you even allow yourself to get scared or can you put it out of your mind completely when you're starting a project like this?

BL: People say to me, "My God, you're so brave," and all that. And I'm just thinking, "What are you talking about?" I'm sort of like, well, gee, somebody's got to make the musical work now. I guess I'll have to do that job, you know?

On the other hand, it would be a lie not to say that every morning I wake up with a sort of sick feeling in my stomach as I think about what we're doing. But it's usually just about making the day work. It's like, "Oh my god, I've got three hundred shots. I'll never get there." It's not an issue for me whether or not a billion people go off to see this movie or only the crowds that are now lining up in L.A. and New York.

In terms of bringing back the musical, for me there's no question that the genie is out of the bottle. I never doubted for a minute that that was going to happen, sooner or later. If it wasn't me, it was going to be someone else. So I'm like, "What's the big deal?" How many absolutely monolithic heads of monolithic companies in the last four days are going, "You know, this is a billion-dollar idea. We own music companies. We own film companies. You bring the two together and they work? Hmmmm." [laughs] It's not rocket science to work out that the world goes around in circles and that this, at some point, was going to come around again.

TK: Given the fact that the movie musical had been considered a dead genre by the major studios for so long, did it take a lot of convincing on your part to get the green light from Fox?

BL: No. In the old days maybe it would have. But just think, I've made a film about ballroom dancing and a film about Shakespeare. Nobody was knocking on my door going, "Please, we really need somebody to make a ballroom dancing film. We know it's going to be huge." or "Shakespeare! That's a great idea!" But they made a lot of money and won a lot of awards.

So you either want the Bazmark thing or you don't. Bazmark Films has a deal now at Fox. I went in and just basically outlined in words the idea for *Moulin Rouge!* and they said, "Not a cent over $45 million. Come back when it's ready." And to be really honest, as much as I'd like to go into a kind of horror story about the studio, the real truth is that they've been unbelievably, relentlessly supportive, like at a ludicrous level.

People lose their jobs over squandering $50 million on having a crack at the musical. But they were the ones who said, "Hey, we think this is a summer picture." I was a little bit more like, "Art-house September looks good to me." They're the ones who went, "This is something for everybody. This can play broad." And, you know, if they believe in my commitment, I've got to believe in their commitment.

We're very family-orientated, in the sense that we work with the same people over a long period of time. And I know it sounds corny but I feel really great that all the people at that studio feel really proud about the achievement of this film. The studio gets a real boost when they actually hear people saying, "Oh, you're doing something edgy. Must be great to work there." It makes Fox an interesting place to be.

TK: While you were working in theater, was it always a goal to cross over into films?

BL: You know, I made movies as a kid and I made plays. It's never been any different for me. I've always made little movies and I've acted in movies and I've acted in plays and I've made records. We come from a small country, Australia, so everybody does a little bit of everything. You've got to. [laughs]

Baz Luhrmann: The Ringmaster

John Lahr / 2002

The Australian director Baz Luhrmann is an impresario of himself; inevitably, for a protean talent, he is known by many names. At the entrance to his temporary base of operations, in a wood-beamed loft on Wooster Street, in New York, he lists himself as "C von G." It's an abbreviation for Count von Groovy, a nickname conferred on Luhrmann by his cohorts, in acknowledgment of both his sometimes grandiose pursuit of the extraordinary and his image as a swami of style. His more common moniker, "Baz," which Luhrmann, who is forty, started using in the seventies—he was christened Mark—is also intended to add a defiant luster to a lifetime of self-invention. "I imagined I needed a fabulous name, an exotic name," he explains. "I was always theatrical. I was mythologizing my own existence from the age of ten." His long-time associate director, David Crooks, agrees. "He likes to see himself as a sort of director cum rock star," he says. "He is the consummate actor. It's very rare that he just takes off all his facades."

Luhrmann has been in town to oversee a production of Puccini's *La Bohème*, which he first staged twelve years ago, at the Sydney Opera House, for $16,000, and which will open on December 8, in a $6.5 million Broadway version. His company Bazmark Inq.—which has its headquarters in a rambling Victorian mansion known as the House of Iona, in Sydney's seedy Kings Cross area—employs about twenty people, including an archivist, but Luhrmann is the source from which the energy flows. He is the visionary, the director, the huckster who pitches the product. "He is the fire," says Luhrmann's wife and partner, Catherine Martin, whose job it is to give his imaginings material form. (Last year, she won two Academy Awards, for the costumes and for the set design of his film, *Moulin Rouge!*) Luhrmann, who has a leading man's good looks and a mane of carefully layered and tinted hair, claims to see "no separation between work and life." For the last thirteen years, he has contrived to be always either in rehearsal, in production, or on the publicity trail. "Work is the prayer," he says. He is, first and foremost, an entrepreneur of astonishment. "It's not enough that you move through the world— you must change it to suit your expectation," he says. The root of his romanticism, he adds, is "a belief that things are better, more incredible, more wonderful than they actually are."

Over the last decade, Luhrmann has produced three flamboyant films that turned into box-office hits: *Strictly Ballroom, Romeo + Juliet,* and *Moulin Rouge!* His movies are distinctive for both their speed and their sharpness. He says, "You've got to create some sort of experience where the audience goes, 'Gee, I feel aggressed, oppressed, but I'm excited.' It cannot be passive." He adds, "Stories never change. The way we tell them must change, so that we can re-enliven the ears and the eyes of the audience." So far, his audiences have been outspoken. *Strictly Ballroom,* which is reported to be one of the Pope's favorite movies, merges the David and Goliath and Ugly Duckling myths in a high-spirited and genial musical about competitive dancing. Luhrmann's deconstruction of Shakespeare, which updates *Romeo and Juliet* to the Miami gang wars, was controversial but won high praise from such actors as Sir Alec Guinness, who admired its "powerful visual imagery." Luhrmann hit rougher water with *Moulin Rouge!,* his attempt to reinvent the Hollywood musical; the film is an acrylic version of the fin-de-siecle in Paris, souped up with cartoonish characters and an eclectic pop score. The response, as noisy as the movie's soundtrack, was divided about evenly between those who called it genius and those who called it a mess. Collectively, the films, which Luhrmann refers to as "tweeners," for their ability to appeal to the art house and the multiplex, have grossed $343 million, and they were recently released in a DVD boxed set as *The Red Curtain Trilogy*—a reference to the theatricality of Luhrmann's cinematic language. He has also moonlighted as guest editor of *Australian Vogue.* In 1999, he produced the spoken-word single, "Everybody's Free (to Wear Sunscreen)," which went platinum in the United States and Britain. And in 2003 he will embark on what he calls his "next big gesture": a film of the life of Alexander the Great.

Bazmark Inq., which Luhrmann founded in 1997, is a sort of artistic holding company for his overheated imagination, with divisions for film, live entertainment, music, and publishing. The company's office is a hive of workers with whom Luhrmann has "a chemical connection," and whose storytelling talents maximize the impact of his work. Bazmark's coat of arms—an emu and a kangaroo—signals a certain lightness of spirit. Its motto—"A life lived in fear is a life half-lived"—broadcasts daring. Part Barnum and part Diaghilev, Luhrmann is also something of an imperialist. He controls the look of every poster, every sign, every piece of information connected to each of his shows, because, as he says, "you're already in the show, even before you've bought a ticket." In the age of the multinational corporation, he aspires to go beyond fame to trademark. "He does want the whole world to be affected by Baz Luhrmann," Crooks says. "To be in people's minds, to make them aware of the Bazmark product." He adds, "He's a humble person in a ruthlessly aggressive way."

When I met Luhrmann in San Francisco in September, *La Boheme* was having its last studio rehearsal before moving from the Presidio Army barracks, near the Golden Gate Bridge, to the Curran Theatre. (It would run for six weeks there, and then travel to New York.) Luhrmann has a quick, conceptualizing mind, and it's sometimes hard to follow him as he bushwhacks his way through a tangle of articulation to a new thought. But, with actors on the rehearsal floor, he is kind, clear, and to the point. He is intense but measured; he rarely yells. His way of registering irritation at the cacophony of cell phones in the vast rehearsal room, for instance, was to say to the assembled, "Would I be wrong in saying there is one too many telephones on today?" (His company runs the same way, in accordance with a book of protocols that Luhrmann has developed, "The Bazmark Way," to keep his artistic domain fair and efficient.)

His work is presentational; his direction, like a brass rubbing, attempts to make vivid and exact the outline of action. "You should actually be able to turn the sound off and follow the story," he says. To his Rodolfo, who on an impulse had carried the frail, consumptive Mimi to her garret chair and dumped her into it, he said, "Lead her into the chair. Like, 'I'm not trying to impose myself on you.' Find what that tells you. This is really a big moment. Stop and listen. Make it a big moment. When you're dealing with Mimi, she is the only purpose for you." Rehearsing the beginning of Act IV, when Colline and Schaunard arrive onstage with their paltry repast of bread and a single silvery fish, Luhrmann spent nearly an hour making a proper spectacle of the scene. "You're showing each other, but you're really sharing it with us," he said of Colline revealing his small catch. Here he imitated Colline flapping the fish matter-of-factly in his friend's direction, and said, "At the moment, it looks like fish, fish, fish, fish. There's no story." He added, "Just lean back in the chair and really connect with the fish moment." By the time he'd moved on to the next bit of low comedy, the fish business had been polished to a shine. "I'm the mechanic," he says. "I'm making the mechanism so the audience can have an experience."

Luhrmann maintains that he is "culturally blind." He says, "I refuse to be drawn into the belief that there is high culture and low culture. There are just things that travel through time and geography." (He, of course, hopes to be one of them.) He often invokes as icons of popular entertainment Shakespeare, Puccini, Moliere, and Mozart, whose "absolute direct connection with the audience" he tries to emulate. Shakespeare, he says, "was singularly driven by the popular environment and by commercial realities. He knew he had to come from a personal place but then decode it, in a way in which the child, the adult, the Queen of England could read it." He adds, "That forced a form of genius."

In order to reach across classes and ages with his own flashy intelligence, Luhrmann chooses simple, mythic stories, which he can update in order to make their subliminal emotional essence accessible. "My mission is to make people feel first, so that they can think, as opposed to making them think so that they can feel," he says, adding, "Psychological work is a fairly recent fashion. We actively reject the idea of psychological depth in character. We have overt archetypal character, overt archetypal story, so that you can have an exalted experience that is individual to you. My job is to vibe the zeitgeist and work out a way of releasing the power of the story."

Luhrmann's productions reflect the thin air of contemporary atmospheres. They conjure a garish, whirligig world that is almost giddy with a combination of doom and delight. The eclecticism of a media-saturated civilization comes through in a collision of fragments, filling the screen with print and image. Luhrmann's organizing principle is, he says, "collage, really: it's basically drawing from any source to make a bigger statement." Martin and Luhrmann create "pitch books" for each of their projects, in order to map out a visual ground plan and explain it to actors and producers. In a book for *Moulin Rouge!*, the hero, Christian, is captioned: "He's multi-talented, he's a genius, he's got the modern technique." Design, not depth, is Luhrmann's dominion. He mines the surface of his stories. Inevitably, therefore, *Romeo + Juliet* overlooks the poorly managed verse; and *Moulin Rouge!*, on first viewing, for me, anyway, was all surprise and no outcome. In order to find a simulacrum for the momentum of turn-of-the-century Paris, Luhrmann paced the movie to "the absolute extreme edge of what we felt the tempo could be and be comprehended." I found the film, with its constant quotations from classic musicals and its cinematic jaggedness, confounding. The old musicals were about flow and the feel of humanity; *Moulin Rouge!* is about interruption and the feel of technology. What you get is sensation without joy. In subsequent screenings, this approach—no pauses, no paths, no future—seemed to me a bold attempt to elevate a claustrophobic style to the level of metaphor. The smash cuts, cross-cuts, zooms and sudden focus shifts, the idiosyncratic soundtrack, the juxtaposition of tragedy and comedy all help to create a roaring—some would say maddening—cinematic language that nonetheless personifies the hellish interior space of contemporary life: what art critic John Berger, speaking of Bosch's vision of hell, calls "the clamour of the disparate, fragmentary present . . . a kind of spatial delirium."

Luhrmann finds a special visual vocabulary for each event. In his *La Boheme*, the opera is sung in Italian and performed in its entirety, but the story has been updated to Paris in 1957. And he has chosen to work against the typical operatic casting, by hiring young, attractive singers, who are believably sexual, to tell the story of starving artists and doomed love. (There are three sets of star-crossed lovers, because eight Broadway performances a week would be too vocally demanding for one couple. "I feel like an acrobat in a Chinese opera who spins plates on the tip of a stick," Luhrmann has said.) To free the production from its traditional naturalistic sedateness, Luhrmann has set the interior scenes in what looks like a revolving Rubik's Cube, pushed around by stagehands who are always visible to the audience, and he makes the supertitles a prominent scenic element by putting them inside the proscenium, not above or below it. "There's no curtain," he explains as the artist's garret is rolled on to its marks. "You walk in. People will be working onstage, singers warming up. Noise. The stage manager—if I can get the lass to embrace it properly—she'll be miked. You'll hear all her calls. She'll just go, 'Stand by,' and there'll be silence. The conductor will come on. She'll say, 'Thank you.' And—bang!—we'll go. You're on. So the curtain is created by the performance." (This has been slightly modified for the Broadway production.)

The maneuver takes the odor off the opera's romanticism. Far from diminishing the power of the music, Luhrmann insists, the emphasis on artifice makes viewers more receptive to the emotional weight of the story. "We show them our hands," he explains. "We say, 'Listen, just so you know, we're here to manipulate you and show you beautiful things. Apparently, you want to do this. Now do you want to be massaged?'" Where naturalism encourages a kind of passivity—"looking through a keyhole" Luhrmann calls it—his "real artificiality" draws the audience into the spirit of play. "You have to teach the audience the story as quickly as possible," he says—thus the gigantic neon sign hanging over the set that reads "L'Amour." "This is not a psychological drama where we're hiding plot. We tell you the plot, so that, as you accumulate tempo, you're breaking down and uniting the audience." He continues, "If you compare, for instance the tempo of Pavarotti's *La Boheme*, which is gorgeous, to Toscanini, who conducted the original production, the original is much faster, because he was telling it to the groundlings—a gutsy romp, a fast comic story, ripping along at the speed of life."

Luhrmann, who is expert at staging entrances and exits, made a dramatic entrance of his own on life's stage. He was born in the back seat of a gray-green Vanguard van, in which his mother was being rushed to the hospital. The ringleader of four siblings, he learned the business of show at his family's Mobil gas station, nine hours into the Australian bush from Sydney. His parents, Leonard and Barbara, had paid $23,000 for a windswept place at a crossroads called Herons Creek, a conurbation of eleven houses on the edge of the Watagan Forest. Luhrmann likens it to the diner in the film *Baghdad Café*—a solitary center of activity in the middle of nowhere. "My relationship with the audience is the same relationship that we had with our customers, that my father drummed into us," says Luhrmann, who pumped gas, waited tables, and ran a tropical-fish concession on the side. "They were our guests. We had to perform. The audience came in every day. We were the Luhrmann Boys. We had to dress up, wear little ties, white shirts, and suits." As cars rolled into the station, they were barraged by a loop of music—the Beatles, the Tijuana Brass, and *Pagliacci*—endlessly repeated over reel-to-reel Akai speakers. Later, his father set up a radio station, and Luhrmann would disk-jockey: "Let's hear that *Pagliacci* one more time!"

Luhrmann calls his parents "an extremely intense couple, huge characters." Both were dreamers, in their own ways charismatic and self-dramatizing. Barbara, in her later years, became a ballroom-dancing instructor. According to Luhrmann, she "always thought she had a light—she had good access to fantasy." Leonard, who served in Vietnam as the head diver of the Australian Navy's demolition squad and as an underwater photographer, was a series of contradictions: soldier-like and soft; disciplined and romantic; practical and problematic. "I think he could love

Baz in a way that his mum couldn't, because he was more true to himself," says the Australian actress Catherine McClements, who lived with Luhrmann and collaborated with him for seven years in the early eighties. Barbara, she adds, was "too busy creating her own life and having her own sort of experiences."

Although the Luhrmanns were just scratching out a living, they were determined to turn out extraordinary offspring. "We were brought up to believe that we were super-special, that there was nothing we couldn't do," Luhrmann says. ("The Renaissance men of Herons Creek" is how Catherine Martin characterizes the family.) "According to their father, you had to be the best," Barbara says. "Their father never really became top of anything he did. He was a good instructor." Leonard, who died of cancer while Luhrmann was shooting *Moulin Rouge!*, oversaw his sons' development in an almost military manner. He insisted on crew cuts, which set the boys apart. "This made our life hell," says Luhrmann, for whom hair remains "a touchstone obsession." "We three boys were constantly attacked and ridiculed. If you had short hair, you were uncool, a freak." Leonard also kept them on a regimen of activities, which included horseback riding, scuba diving, farm and gas-station chores, commando training—"He'd drop us in the middle of the bush and we had to find our way home"—and competitive ballroom dancing, which meant a three-hour drive, three days a week. "One of the great things his parents gave him was no fear of mastering physical challenges," Martin says. By the age of ten, Luhrmann also knew how to develop the negatives of the photographs he took with his first camera, a Brownie, and how to operate his father's Straight 8 Bolex moving-picture camera. (Luhrmann made *Strictly Ballroom* without any additional cinematic tutelage.) "There was never a moment of peace," he says of the "almost psychotic" amount of childhood activity. "If we ever just sat down, the sense from my father was that it was wrong. We weren't allowed to eat until dinner. We had work to do. It was absolutely non-stop until we dropped at night. We got up early in the morning, and—bang!—you'd do it again." He adds, "My family was a cult."

Luhrmann's mercurial quality and his fertile fantasy life ("I imagine twenty-four hours a day—it's like a storm," he says) seem to derive from the habit of ducking and diving he adopted as a child, in order to evade his parents' control. "Both parents had tyrannical natures," Martin says. Leonard imposed himself; Barbara exerted her power by withdrawing. "Baz got out of things by being incredibly entertaining," Martin adds. "He was always in his head, maybe because he thought he wasn't fabulous enough. He had to create it." In person and in public, Luhrmann accentuates the positive aspects of his tense, hard-striving childhood. But no one courts fame out of happiness. "There was a lot of shadow, sure," he admits. "We lived daily with death. We lived on a bridge, which on a regular basis caused car accidents that killed people. My job was to man the phone or call the local cop. Violence was around. The level of drama was extreme." But, when pushed to speak about the shadows in his own life, Luhrmann struggles to find language. His long silence surprises him. "I'm never at a loss for words, as you know," he says. What he can't bring himself to acknowledge is that, for part of his childhood—until he was ten, according to his mother—the man whom he now thinks of as "a wonderful father" was an alcoholic, and that by his teenage years the family atmosphere, according to his mother, was "dreadful." "Their father was too hard, too harsh, almost impossible to live with," Barbara says. Leonard sometimes wouldn't speak to her for three weeks at a time. "Fifteen years. I couldn't take it anymore." Their break-up was violent and traumatic. "It was a horrendous day," Luhrmann recalls. "There were many horrendous days. There was my sister and a lamp shade in a car. And screaming and hitting and yelling. And she was gone."

Luhrmann remained with his father at Herons Creek, nursing subversive longings for the big city and, he says, "aware that we were perhaps incarcerated in this other world." After about eighteen months, Len remarried; three and a half years later, Luhrmann, then fifteen, ran away. He ended up living in Sydney with his mother and didn't see his father again for seven years. He attended an all-boys Catholic high school, which he found, he says, "a bit of a shock." He rebelled by growing his curly hair long, and he earned the nickname Basil Brush—after a furry fox puppet on British television—which was the derogatory origin of Baz. Around 1979, "as an act of defiance against this derision," Luhrmann says, he changed his name officially to Bazmark. "Baz and Mark are the two sides of who I am," he says.

Luhrmann was not an outstanding student, but he was drawn to acting. (He played Sky Masterson in a high-school production of *Guys and Dolls*.) "I can remember walking back from the beach, the heat coming off the road, and Baz talking about great acting and great theater and great movies, and wanting to be great," the screenwriter Craig Pearce says. (Pearce, who was Luhrmann's best friend in high school, is the co-author of all three of his films.) He adds, "What I was attracted to in Baz was this feeling of being part of something bigger. It was going to happen." Pearce and Luhrmann didn't aspire to be jobbing actors; they wanted to be, as Pearce puts it, "Marlon Brando, Montgomery Clift, James Dean, Mick Jagger, all rolled into one." He says of Luhrmann, "He wanted to be extraordinary and, in a sense, when you were around Baz life was more extraordinary." For Luhrmann, acting was a natural direction; he had been role-playing all his life. "In order to avoid confrontation, he would become whatever was asked of him," his mother says.

Luhrmann applied to Sydney's National Institute of Dramatic Art, "the grand temple of serious acting," he calls it. He was rejected, but on the same day he received word that he'd been cast as a pimp, playing opposite Judy Davis in *Winter of Our Dreams*. He was eighteen. He went straight from high school to a full-fledged acting career. He was featured in one of Australia's most popular television shows, *A Country Practice*, and had a convincing cameo as a transsexual on another show. For a documentary he conceived about Sydney's homeless youth—*Kids from the Cross*—he shed his suburban looks, went undercover, and slept rough for three months. When Luhrmann couldn't find financing for the film, he took the footage to a television company, which turned it into an embarrassing program that left him "morally confused" and brought him into the unfortunate glare of Australia's tabloid press. "HOW KIDS SURVIVE IN A CESSPOOL—THIS IS SICK" was the headline in one Sydney paper. The result, he says, was "a very, very, very strong drive to be creatively responsible." Prodded also by the fact that "sitting around waiting for the phone to ring was basically killing me," he formed his first theatre company, The Bond, in 1981.

At twenty, Luhrmann was accepted at the National Institute of Dramatic Art. By his own admission, he became "internalized, self-conscious, very intense." He says, "I have always had a natural connection with people. But I think I read that as uncool and not what serious artists did. I was very unapproachable." He cultivated a sense of mystery and danger. "People imagined that he was uncontrollable, that he was scary, that he broke the rules," Catherine McClements says. Luhrmann did his best not to disappoint. To act Chekhov, he studied Russian; to play a Chinese peasant in *Fanshen*, David Hare's play about Communist Chinese agrarian reform, he walked around with his books in a pail and put his fist through a window, trying to pull a punch. "I created a character who wasn't me," he says. He explored the postures and attitudes of Elvis, Nijinsky, David Bowie, and Prince. Obsessed by African American culture, Luhrmann even turned up for one class as a black woman. "He was incredibly convincing," McClements says. "One time, we were listening to classical music. He said, 'You've really gotta forgive me for this.'

He went off, and that night at the corroboree"—an Aboriginal word for gathering—"he dressed up as an opera singer, with the whole gear, lip-synching way before it became popular. The drag was brilliantly done."

McClements helped Luhrmann develop *Strictly Ballroom*, which began life as an acting-school exploration and a metaphor for, among other things, his increasing sense of "creative oppression" at NIDA. "I'm sick of dancing someone else's steps," the hero of *Strictly Ballroom* says, before he finds a way to triumph on his own terms. When Luhrmann entered NIDA, he had an acting career, an agent, his own theater company; when he left, he had nothing. "He entered drama school as a fantastic actor and through the process at NIDA became worse and worse," McClements says. "He became too self-aware." He felt stalled. He was frightened. "Things weren't going to plan," Luhrmann says. "I had a genuine breakdown." For about a month, he sat paralyzed in the squalor of a ramshackle fishing hut, barely moving or speaking. Finally, one day, he remembers, he walked to the beach, ate a popsicle, and started to read the paper. "I suddenly thought, I'm going to do something—I'm going to put on a play," he says. "I got my old company back and convinced everyone I could do this production, *About the Beach*, a sort of myth set in the beach culture of lifeguards and surfing. From that day on, I was back to being who I was before I went to NIDA."

Luhrmann likes to tell the story of his first screening at Cannes, in 1992, with *Strictly Ballroom*. "I remember every second of it," he says. "Nervously hanging up signs: 'Come and see our film.' A very small audience coming to see it, then a standing ovation. Then us being the toast of the town. Twenty-four hours later, another screening being called—you couldn't get in. A security guard leaned over and said to me, 'Monsieur, your life will never be the same again.'" So it has proved. Fame is a live wire that Luhrmann can't let go of. "You can't shake it off at the flick of a switch," he says. "You can't go home. Your home is the public world." Now he lives at full tilt. "If I'm able to run the movie of my life, in my mind it'd better be a good one," he says. "You can't afford any sloppy scenes."

Luhrmann is built for speed. He's thin, lithe, and streamlined, rejecting anything that might weigh him down. His collaboration with Martin has only increased his velocity. From the outset, for Luhrmann, artistic partnership was crucial to creative success. "He definitely needs someone to be in love with him, to be obsessed with him and what he's doing, and to make him feel good about it," McClements says. "He doesn't want to be alone." Martin was a designer in her third year at NIDA when, in 1986, Luhrmann discovered her and she joined his opera and theater companies. Her first real memory of Luhrmann, though, came a year later, when they were working together on *Lake Lost*, an opera he was directing. "He had two stage managers pushing this rowboat on wheels with two of the lead players inside. I just remember thinking that this man was a fucking genius. It was so beautifully artificial." She adds, "What Baz forces you to do is go through the cliche to a transcendental understanding."

Of their at-times volatile early relationship, she says, "We connected in a profound way. It was more than romantic love or sexual attraction. It was bigger and more frightening than that. He not only channels himself through the collaboration, he pulls out the best in you." She adds, "He's the magic, but I'm the high priestess." Luhrmann and Martin were married at a Sydney registry office in 1997. In the post-wedding celebration, Martin, who is thirty-seven and known as C.M., literally ascended to her new role on the stage of the Sydney Opera House, where *La Bohème* had played. There, under the "L'Amour" sign, in a notional chapel made of candles, she rose into the scene on a hydraulic lift as the producer Noel Staunton, who now heads Bazmark's live-entertainment division, descended from above in an angel costume, to officiate in yet another Baz Luhrmann spectacle.

In the vortex of his production and promotion schedules, one way that Luhrmann stops time is to keep a diary. The frontispiece of each year's journal, which is about the size of an accounting ledger, is a photograph of his current project; the back cover shows his next one. Instead of writing about his hectic life, he fills the diary pages with a visual record: images and mementos snatched from the blur of hours, which reflect him back to himself. The quick inventory I compiled, as I flipped through his 2002 diary during a production meeting, included:

January 15: Luhrmann asleep on C.M.'s lap. A letter from Martin Scorsese.

January 21: The Golden Globe Awards: Luhrmann stands with Nicole Kidman on a red carpet, Luhrmann and C.M. reclining in deck chairs on their hotel patio. Hair unkempt, unshaven, Luhrmann looks hungover. C.M. holds up an ad in the *L.A. Times*: "3 Winners: Best Picture, Best Actress, Best Original Score."

February 14: A card from Kidman: "She sings, she dances, she dies. . . . Thank you for giving me the gift of a lifetime. Nic."

March 5: Luhrmann with Debbie Reynolds and Carrie Fisher.

March 24: Ticket stubs to the 74th Academy Awards—Center B-1. A photo of Rupert Murdoch holding one of C.M.'s Academy Awards; C.M. stands beaming beside him with the other Oscar.

May 10: India—a map of the state of Kerala.

Years, for Luhrmann, are measured not by days but by work, and his chronicle consists mostly of lists. "When I get hugely insecure, I make lists and lists and lists of things I have to do," he says. The 2002 diary began with a list of "goals." Among them were "Conceive a child" and "ISSUE—I am exhausted and fucked trying to conceive and develop *Boheme.*"

Luhrmann's diary is symptomatic of something essential in his performing nature: he is always watching himself go by. "It's not vanity as we understand it," McClements says. "It's experimenting with himself." "He spends a lot of time looking at himself in the mirror," Crooks says. Luhrmann, who, like the characters in *Strictly Ballroom*, was a ballroom-dancing champion as a boy, believes in looking good. He doesn't allow the cast to see him eat, and, before he goes on the rehearsal floor, if there is anyone from the press around, he often spends a few minutes in Hair and Makeup. (The stated Four Pillars of the House of Iona are "Transportation, Communication, Accommodation, and Hair." "Over the years, I've learned that these four elements are the ones to watch out for in derailing the creative process," he explains.) According to Crooks, "If there's a photo to be done, there's just a little touch of something, a little Aschenbach moment." Still, his self-regard has nothing to do with looking inward. "Only look out," he advises. Like his films, he resists psychology. "I put my own character off-limits for a very long time," he explains. Luhrmann recalls listening to Leonardo DiCaprio, who starred in *Romeo + Juliet*, do impersonations. "He's a fantastic impersonator," he says. "We're sitting in a circle. We're laughing at his Johnny Depp, Robert De Niro—great. Marlon Brando. And he does another one. Everybody's laughing, laughing, laughing. And I'm going, 'Oh, who is it?'" Luhrmann says, "It was me."

When we sat down to talk alone, during a rehearsal break, on what turned out to be Luhrmann's fortieth birthday, September 17, he was considering the nature of his self-invention. "Is it that I construct a life that seems to be tremendously well stage-managed?" he asked. "Or is it that my zealous romanticism has caused a very interesting staging of my life? The curtain is coming down on the first act of my life. It's ending with the production I began with, thirteen years ago." He added, "I'm not young anymore. And I'm gonna be old. The new journey is a spiritual one." Later, in front of the cast and crew, who presented him with wine and proffered a birthday cake with a burst of song—"Couldn't we get decent singers to sing me *Happy Birthday*?" Luhrmann said—he feigned surprise. "I couldn't think of a better way of turning forty than just to be in the middle of doing *La Boheme*. With such risk out there, with all of you." He went on, "If you turn forty, the thing that everyone talks about is you feel your life's over. I just feel like I'm right in the middle of life. I am very, very privileged. Well, listen, look: I'll tell you what"—here he looked at the cake and then at his watch. "Beautiful, but the show must go on."

Although the three films of "The Red Curtain Trilogy" are devoted to the conventions of traditional narrative and heterosexual love, the camp style of Luhrmann's telling always subverts normality. This contradiction seems to express what McClements calls his "uncertain heart." He seems almost obsessed with the romantic entanglements of others. "For somebody who's not an overtly sexual being, he loves watching people in love," Crooks says. Luhrmann admits that his fascination with Romeo and Juliet was about "coming to terms with an impossible love, which could not be, no matter how perfect." When he talks about *Alexander the Great*, his preoccupation with love seems to reveal the autobiography beneath the archetype. "I'm thinking of doing a work about a young historical figure who must continually succeed and conquer because of a lack of love, because he is pursuing a phantom love," Luhrmann told San Francisco's *Bay Area Reporter*. "He goes on and on until there can be no more conquering, and at a certain point you've got to realize that that phantom love will never be found."

After *La Boheme* opens on Broadway, and before Luhrmann gets into the heavy lifting of *Alexander the Great*, he will do what he always does at the end of an epic undertaking: go walkabout. "I never know where I'm going," says Luhrmann, who ended up in Alexandria on his last sojourn. He will turn up at the airport, he will put his credit card on the counter, and, except for a few calls home during the couple of months away, he will get lost on the planet. "One gets connected to the street, to the world, to life," he says. "I think it's absolutely fundamental because that's the audience." He also reconnects to his own romantic notion of "the wandering storyteller." In this persona, he is a denizen of the underworld, albeit a Prada bohemian, a pilgrim in search of an answer to some longing he can't quite bring himself to define. One night over dinner in San Francisco, talking about Alexander the Great, Luhrmann almost found the words. "He needed love from everyone," he told me. "The love of the army, the love of Hephaestion, the love of Roxanne. I understand without any complication what it is to feel the need."

Baz Luhrmann

Harvey Kubernik / 2006

Interscope Records released the soundtrack, *Music from Baz Luhrmann's Film, Moulin Rouge!*, the 20th Century Fox movie.

Previously, the Australian-born Luhrmann directed *Romeo + Juliet* and *Strictly Ballroom*. He had also released on CD *Something for Everybody (Music from the House of Iona)*, a collection of remixed and reinterpreted songs from his films, theater, and opera, including hits from *Romeo + Juliet, Strictly Ballroom,* and *La Boheme.*

Moulin Rouge! stars Nicole Kidman, Ewan McGregor, John Leguizamo, Jim Broadbent, and Richard Roxburgh. It was written by Luhrmann and Craig Pearce.

Current cutting-edge artists, lyricists, and composers collaborated closely with writer-director Luhrmann on this soundtrack. *Moulin Rouge!* is a period piece musical, underscored with elements of comedy and tragedy, a merger of love and inspiration set in 1900, in the infamous Paris nightclub. Luhrmann threads together text, narration, and speech with modern-era pop tunes, and celebrates many key pop songs of the twentieth century, from Rodgers and Hammerstein to Lennon and McCartney, from Sting to Elton John, from Dolly Parton, Bob Crewe, and Jack Nitzsche to David Bowie.

Bowie sings Eden Ahbez's "Nature Boy," initially made famous by Nat King Cole, and reprises it as well with Massive Attack, with the song bookending the compilation. Fatboy Slim offers a new tune, "Because We Can," for the film. Bono, Gavin Friday, and Maurice Seezer cover T-Rex's/Marc Bolan's "Children of the Revolution." Jose Feliciano and actors McGregor and Jacek Koman team to create a tango version of the Police's "Roxanne," mixed with a classic Argentine tango, "Tanguera," by Mariano Mores. There are other tunes aired in the movie, including some not available in the soundtrack package. Nicole Kidman and Ewan McGregor make their on-screen and soundtrack singing debuts.

Harvey Kubernik: It seems that your earlier *Something for Everybody (Music from the House of Iona)* album had an impact on *Moulin Rouge!* and the subsequent soundtrack album. Narration, spoken word, reinterpreted songs from opera?

Baz Luhrmann: You know what? It's a good observation and it's real simple. Anton Monsted, my music supervisor, also co-produced a lot of the tracks on the *Music from the House of Iona* album with me. We set out to do that as a practice run for doing *Moulin Rouge!* Specifically, we were going to do a little charity record for Australia. We wanted to do more hands-on producing, because, with all the films I've done, I work very closely on the music, and I worked closely on *Romeo + Juliet* with Nellee Hooper, Marius de Vries, and Craig Armstrong, to actually physically produce the music myself and to do that hands-on work. So I was ready. And, also, this way we could deal with the eclectic nature of the music that was going to be used in *Moulin Rouge!* So that was the starting point.

HK: The hit, "Everybody's Free (to Wear Sunscreen)": a year after release in the U.K., it pops stateside. Did you know when it was first recorded that you had something special? Didn't some people, or music and record industry ears, think you were off your rocker, or doing something out of format?

BL: As with all the music that we do, y'know, Harvey, every record I've ever made, including the album for *Romeo + Juliet*, I had a lot of A&R people telling me, "That will never work in the states." "It's too different." "It's too eclectic." That was the whole thing with *R+J*: "Too European." The thing is: there's this assumption that because I work in Australia, it couldn't be the same here.

HK: But this flow and song mix seems very logical and natural. Is it always a fight?

BL: No-one has ever asked me this before, and, yes, it is always a fight. Going back to the first part of your question: yes, it's quite natural to me. It is really the way we see the world. I've grown up in a very isolated place. I love music. Just great music, whether it's rap, opera, or rock, and the universality of things, is what attracts me, not the division.

The thought of the need for economics is the strongest in the States.

I don't mean that as a criticism, just as an acknowledgement of how difficult it is, when it's such a vast market, to segregate things, to focus things, to nail and nail and nail. And so, therefore, it has turned into a fight, and it's a fight I've had from my very first film.

Romeo + Juliet sold eight million copies worldwide. "This soundtrack is too eclectic," they told me when I first talked to EMI about the marketing. Then it went multiplatinum. You know what I mean? I've got to tell you, though, it's been the reverse at Interscope.

HK: You had made two films before *Moulin Rouge!*: *Romeo + Juliet* and *Strictly Ballroom.*
BL: Do you think any executive was begging me to make those films?
HK: No.
BL: Exactly. With the second, it was kind of like, "William Shakespeare!? Go back to the ballroom dancing. We know that can be a hit." Eventually the film becomes a Bazmark Production: "As long as he doesn't go off his number, what do we know about reinventing the musical?" Y'know?

With *Moulin Rouge!*, we are using traditional break-out-into-song techniques, Greek chorus techniques, post-mod MTV techniques, and some of our own techniques.

HK: You are blending a lot of dialogue, speech and text, music and songs, and along the way you are giving some well-deserved props to the writers and lyricists. It's refreshing to hear on the big screen. So why can't narrative and speech and song be more in demand in film projects?
BL: It matters to me. People say, "Oh, you're so daring." But I'm very much of the mind of, "Daring? I'm just saying it's just a natural step. It's going to happen, even if I don't do it." You can feel it around you; think of people like Dre and people like that, who are reaching their tentacles out for film, or people who write poetry, or spoken word.

This is going to be the last of the "red curtain" films I make, although I will do music cinema again. But sometime next year I want to see a film where someone is using a spoken-word or rap-like storytelling in cinema. It's got to happen. It's going to happen.

That's why we've got audiences who clap and cheer at the songs in cinemas. They are not cheering the projectionist. What they are doing is communing with everybody else in the room and saying, "Ha ha ha. I get it too." You know: "We're unified by this experience." Now nothing is more powerful than that in doing music. If you can shackle music to story, not shackle, but display music through story, I know it sounds dramatic, but if you can do that, you unleash a force that is unstoppable. I feel that *Moulin Rouge!* is just the first step on that road.

HK: One of your central goals then obviously is to move the story along with music.

BL: That's a rule. If you break that rule you are in dire trouble. The music is only there to advance the plot, and I had many musical ideas that had to be jettisoned simply because they weren't advancing plot or revealing character.

HK: You've also mentioned that, when making *Moulin Rouge!*, it was about breaking "the code." It's like a combination of many cinematic languages applied to music numbers.

BL: Well, when I say "breaking the code," what I'm talking about is that we needed to find a code, if you like, to make it acceptable for people to tell story through song in this moment. Now, while we reference the past, and we look to the future, it's ultimately a potpourri of references and techniques that speak to a person now.

It's just about a deal between the film and the audience that allows the contemporary audience to know they are in on it. *Moulin Rouge!* and its particular cinematic form are part of a larger gesture that we started ten years ago and we're concluding now. With the film, we want to do the finest version of this cinematic form.

HK: When you were first writing *Moulin Rouge!*, did you already have certain songs, recording artists, and composers in the initial draft? Did you write the script with definite songs and tunes in place?

BL: This is what happened. I began with a philosophy. Here's the background. First, I wanted to reinvent the musical. Second, I also wanted a musical where the musical language on one hand had to tell story; on the other hand, I wanted the track to it to be eclectic like a modern soundtrack, instead of using one voice. So I just didn't want to work with one voice.

Some background notes, Harvey. It's a very old idea in musicals, like when Judy Garland sings "Clang clang clang went the trolley" in *Meet Me in St. Louis* [1944]. That's set in 1900 and she is singing big band music from the 1940s, the music of her time, to let you into the characters of another time and another place.

The other thing is that, in an old musical, the audience had a relationship to the music generally before they went in, whether it was in a Broadway show or with songs that moved from film to film. So the audience having a pre-existing relationship to at least some of the music was very important. Hence, Craig [Pearce] and I came up with the device of our main character telling the story, and, because he was a poet, channelling, if you like, the great examples of every kind of music of the last hundred years. So that's how we began. Then we constructed a very simple story that took a long time to do, based on a few things including *La Boheme*. And, once we had a recognizable story for the audience, we spent a great deal of time scanning, scanning, and scanning songs to identify which one would best tell a particular moment or reveal a character.

HK: Did "Nature Boy" set the tone early for the film? It's used twice on the available soundtrack, opening and closing the disc.
BL: Actually, you know what? I have to tell you honestly that was the one song that came a little later in the process. Eden Ahbez is an Orphic, messianic character. I've always loved "Nature Boy," but when I learned about the story of Eden Ahbez, I realized the song reflected the overall structure of the film. And I grew that out during the shooting process.

I'll tell you how it came about. I actually began the film with a theme between the father and the son with Cat Stevens's "Father and Son." What happened was that Cat rejected it, based on religious beliefs. OK, I respect him for that. But that left me wondering, "How do I clarify the structures?" So, coming back to it and having identified the song, then it was about how to get the licensing people to agree. Honestly, it was just a journey of going to see most of the artists one-on-one. I went to publishing companies and they were enthusiastic, because the proposal represented a new use of popular song, in the grand rite of the musical. But then I met with Elton [John]. I knew Bono. I wrote to Paul McCartney. I met with Dolly Parton. They were really enthusiastic. You know, Harvey, if it were the 1940s, someone like Bono would be writing for movie musicals.

No one stood in our way. It was the opposite: because we didn't have that much money. I worked with Bowie quite openly on it. He was very supportive in giving us the song, "Heroes." I've got a lot of codes. Subtle signs and symbols. It's like a record. If you play this movie more than once, you hear things. Bowie appears through it, and I was going to use him with Massive Attack on the end credits. But he and Massive ended up being, in a sense, so dark that we needed to resurrect the audience during the credits. So that's where the idea of "The Bolero" came from, which Steve Hitchcock or then Steve Sharples composed.

I really enjoyed working with Bowie. He was very giving. You can imagine how he feels about the film.

HK: When did songs start entering the scenes on the pages?

BL: They were all driven by one question: "What does the story beat need?" Now, I love "Nature Boy," so I was happy that it revealed itself as the right choice. But things were dropped. We had "Under My Thumb" in a kind of rape scene, but we didn't need it in the end. So I missed a Rolling Stones piece. But it wasn't about, "Well, we must have a Rolling Stones piece." It's a story that simply doesn't need it.

HK: What is the secret of getting and working together with music people, labels, publishers, songwriters, to serve the project? Hassles, games, egos?

BL: Y'know what: the silver sword to cut through all of that is that the idea is so exciting that it actually diminishes all of those fears.

Other than being an acolyte of that, I personally go and—I hope—enthuse people and explain and involve them, and don't manipulate them and don't make them feel that what we're doing is a quickie. Our love of what we're making, which is so absolute, is also about transporting that. And how often do you get the opportunity to actually work on something where you're reinventing a genre or breaking new ground? People really find that exciting.

HK: The film's songwriting credits, and to a lesser extent, the soundtrack, due to space limitations, have so many names you never see linked together. From Paul Stanley of Kiss to Rodgers and Hammerstein. Yet radio programmers, print, and electronic media often fail to integrate their names in broadcasts or magazines in the same pages.

BL: Exactly, exactly. I'm blind to it, Harvey, I'm blind to it. To me, they are all great tunes, great popular culture. Popular culture today becomes classical culture tomorrow. Shakespeare was pop of its time. I work in opera. So I know that Puccini was the television of his time. One of the strengths of the piece is that I am captain of the collaboration. I am very big on collaborators. I wanted all kinds of musical talents to work together.

HK: "Lady Marmalade" is done in the film with four actors, another character is rapping over it with spoken word, and "Teen Spirit" is being sung at the same time. So it's really a round of three things. Much like an opera. Then Paul Hunter directed a video, away from the film, with Christina Aguilera, Lil' Kim, Mya, and Pink.

BL: I think the video is a very good interpretation of the film. It's not the film, but it captures some moments. We supported him a lot, gave him some stuff. The idea was to say, "Look, Paul, don't try to homage the movie. Just go and make a gesture that tells what you got from the film."

HK: "Sparkling Diamonds" features Nicole Kidman's vocals.

BL: Nicole turned out to be a wonderful singer. She tells the story through her voice.

HK: Ewan McGregor has a very pretty singing voice too. Really carries a rendition of "Your Song." I know he worked very hard with a vocal coach, and he can sing. It's a pivotal part in the movie, and I'm sure it helps that your leading man can really carry a note.

BL: Elton John would agree with you. Ewan worked really hard and he grew into a great singer in front of us, really. He was good, but he became great. When Elton saw the footage of Ewan doing "Your Song," he went, "My God, he really is a singer." There's a recording career ahead of him if he so chooses. That's been one of the great surprises, just how strong he is.

HK: His singing was as convincing as Marlon Brando in *Guys and Dolls*.

BL: I totally agree with you and that's a favorite role of mine. But he has got that absolutely bold face openness to the camera, which you have to have to sing. Singing exposes you on a very deep level. You've got to be able to be that vulnerable, open, and exposed.

HK: Then there's a T-Rex song, "Children of the Revolution," that unites Bono, Gavin Friday, and Maurice Seezer. It's one of the important cues in the film and on the soundtrack album. Bolan and T-Rex are overlooked in America.

BL: Marc Bolan is hugely underrated in America. T-Rex is bigger for us in Australia. That was a theme for me, "Children of the Revolution." But also, again, it's all about story. It's about the Bohemians, in a Bohemian revolution. It's about identifying popular songs that can unite all of us, that tell story. It's that simple.

Bono actually rang me about something else. He's such a great supporter of my films and he said, "Anything I can do to help out with *Moulin Rouge!*?" I said, "Well, as a matter of fact . . ." "Maybe I can make a cup of tea." So he went in with Gavin, who worked with us on *Romeo + Juliet*, and Maurice, and he made that track in about a week for us. He was very passionate about it, y'know, as only Bono can be. You're a lucky person if you get to work with Bono, I have to say that.

HK: Was there ever a time when you reviewed songs and tunes and artist pairings, looked at something and felt, this is too obvious, or it telegraphs too much?

BL: No. I think it's really important that you take the obvious. You take what you might think is the "cheesiest," you take something that is overt, and what you do is turn it on its head. Because there is a reason why things are obvious. They have value inside them. The problem is they become rusty from overuse. What we had to do was shake the rust off by inverting it. So I feel that what we've done with that piece is invert it by subjecting it to story. You can constantly shake the rust off. And, you know, anything that survives time and geography is always worth revisiting.

HK: You had a great say in the casting of the movie. Did you initially look for actors that you thought could work vocally as singers?

BL: You know, in my films I have a big say about every single thing. You know what I mean? I looked very extensively—and I'd worked with both Nicole and Ewan before—but I had to find actors that could sing the roles. Ultimately, it sounds boring, but they got the jobs because they were best for them. That's really the truth.

HK: That doesn't happen very often in this world.

BL: Well, no. But, as I say, for all the disadvantages of trying to reinvent the wheel every time we make a movie, one of the advantages is that you're left alone. It's got to be the right person for the right role.

HK: Don't you think some of the songs were better realized when matched with the visual?

BL: Well, yes, I think that's very true. I mean, it's storytelling music. If you were creating it just for a sonic experience, you would probably take different roads on certain tracks.

HK: The film at times attacks the senses.

BL: Yes. Particularly in the first twenty minutes. It's important that I wake people up. It's not a passive experience. It has to slap you around a bit so that, by the time they break out into song, it becomes quite classical. I hope you surrender to the contract.

HK: Even though you didn't get the use of the Cat Stevens principal theme early on, and then "Nature Boy" sort of emerged out of the pack to be featured widely on the soundtrack disc and in the movie, it appears often you find out things happen for a reason. Andrew Loog Oldham once told me, "There are no accidents."

BL: Do you know what? There *are* no accidents. You are going always to the same place. How you get there is your inventiveness.

HK: Ultimately, you are serving the whole in some sort of Zen capacity.

BL: Absolutely. I think the reason for all the crazy ego stuff, the thing that actually makes it a human experience and worthwhile, is that we all finally serve something greater than ourselves. That is the story, the piece you are making. That is the beautiful side of this creative process. What it is, Harvey, is that it is ultimately fulfilling. That, I can say, is the truth.

HK: The film moves comedy and tragedy forward together.

BL: Comedy and tragedy together are not common on our screen, but they should be, because our audience is used to swinging from comedy to tragedy. Now we're so advanced in being aware of manipulation, we can sign the contract that allows us to accept that.

Closing the Red Curtain
with *La Boheme*

Terry Keefe / 2004

From Hollywood Interview (www.theHollywoodInterview.com) and *Venice Magazine*, February 2004. Reprinted by permission of the author.

Before moving on from the cinematic delights of his Red Curtain Trilogy, Baz Luhrmann revisits the Puccini masterwork which kicked off his career. This interview was for the Los Angeles run of *La Boheme* at the Los Angeles Opera.

I first spoke to him in the spring of 2001 [see pp. 78–83], on the eve of the opening of his feature *Moulin Rouge!* He was already a highly accomplished director by any standards, with the box office successes of *Strictly Ballroom* (1992) and *Romeo + Juliet* (1996) under his belt. But *Moulin Rouge!* was a different level of project entirely. Working with his biggest budget to date, $52 million, Luhrmann was attempting to revive the movie musical, a genre that couldn't have been deader at the time. And in what must have caused even more sleepless nights for the studio bean counters, he wasn't doing it in the safest and most conservative manner.

Moulin Rouge! combined the style of traditional movie musicals with every imaginable strain of pop culture to create something very new, a giddy pastiche that was intoxicating as absinthe to some, and a little too much for others. In the days leading up to its release, it was impossible to gauge what critical and popular reaction would be. Studios and careers have fallen many times in the past on daring film projects and *Moulin Rouge!* was as daring as they come.

Knowing full well that positive publicity was going to be a key factor in the film's future, Luhrmann leaped into a barnstorming tour of interviews, seeming to be everywhere at once. Although he was clearly aware of the stakes, he didn't seem to be unnerved at all by them, and that probably shouldn't have been a surprise. After all, this was a man who had previously created a Shakespearean film that teenagers embraced, and he had also made ballroom dancing actually seem cool with his debut picture, *Strictly Ballroom*.

The impression I received was that he was primarily concerned with explaining his bold vision to the prospective audience, hoping to convince them that his magic carpet ride was one worth taking. The audiences agreed that it was. *Moulin Rouge!* would go on to be a smash in every way, grossing $175 million worldwide, receiving eight Academy Award nominations and winning two. The film's influence reached wide in Hollywood, as it unquestionably paved the way for the success of *Chicago* the following year.

The Baz Luhrmann whom I met last month is obviously now in a very different position career-wise from when we first spoke. Having conquered the world with *Moulin Rouge!*, he's a proven commodity on the largest of scales, and investing in his next big undertaking is most likely now seen less as a risk than as a wise decision. And in terms of his creative direction, things are also changing for him. *Moulin Rouge!* was the cinematic culmination of what Luhrmann refers to as his "Red Curtain Trilogy," which began with *Strictly Ballroom*. He's announced that his next film will be the story of Alexander the Great, which will likely be a step in a new aesthetic direction for him. But before he moves on to that next chapter in his filmmaking odyssey, he has decided to return for one final time to the opera which served as a kind of rehearsal for the Red Curtain Trilogy: *La Boheme*.

No, Luhrmann never made a theatrical film of the grand Giacomo Puccini masterpiece, which tells the tale of a doomed love affair between the seamstress, Mimi, and the writer, Rodolfo, in Bohemian Paris.* But it was his production of it in 1990 at the Sydney Opera House which truly began his career and led to the financing of *Strictly Ballroom*. And the spirit with which he and Catherine Martin reinvented the opera is the same one which drove their Red Curtain Trilogy.

It's part of the Baz Luhrmann legend that, when he was first announced as the director of *La Boheme* at the Sydney Opera House in 1990, nine-tenths of the subscribers cancelled. At the time, he was best known as a very experimental theater director. But when the red curtains rose on his production, Luhrmann would quickly silence most of his critics, with the show going on to set box office records in Sydney.

Although he kept many of the traditional elements of the opera in place, Luhrmann updated it in ways which brought the original spirit of the piece back to life. In Puccini's day, opera was the popular entertainment. It was sexy. And in keeping with that, Luhrmann cast attractive twenty-somethings in the leads, while pushing the time period from the 1800s to 1957. The result not only satisfied opera purists, but also introduced a whole new, younger audience to opera for the first time.

In the audience at the Sydney Opera House were the future Broadway producers of *Rent*, who drew inspiration from the production, and more than a decade later convinced Luhrmann to remount *La Boheme* for a Broadway run. Luhrmann went on a worldwide talent search to find the top young opera talent in the business, eventually landing an international cast which alternated shows. Three different performers were cast for both the roles of Mimi and Rodolfo. Amongst the Mimis were Lisa Hopkins from the United States, Ekaterina Solovyeva from Russia, and Wei Huang from China. And the Rodolfos included David Miller and Jesus Garcia from the United States, and Alfred Boe from the United Kingdom.

Opening on December 8, 2002, the new version of *La Boheme* was an instant smash, nominated for six Tony Awards and winning for Best Scenic Design (Catherine Martin) and Best Lighting Design (Nigel Levings). Starting in January, the show will be presented in Los Angeles at the Ahmanson Theatre.

Luhrmann has been doing interviews all day long by the time I see him, but he never seems to tire. Once again, I shouldn't be surprised. Someone looking for the easy way would never have been able to create the vast new worlds which he has been showing us behind his Red Curtain for over a decade now.

Terry Keefe: So does this new staging of *La Boheme* feel like a closing of a circle of sorts for you?

Baz Luhrmann: Yeah, that is why we did it. We did it for two reasons probably. One, I really wanted to live in New York for awhile and stop touring. We're always running around, doing crazy things, which is part of the work that we do. But also, when we originally did *La Boheme*, it was the very beginning of this period of work that the Red Curtain Trilogy, those three films, belonged to. It was the same investigation of style. It was the same idea of taking emotional stories and telling them in a heightened, creative way, right? So as I was moving out of it, and as I was turning forty, and given that, when I first did it, I always said rather arrogantly, as I was an arrogant little thing [laughs], "We don't want to be forty and doing *La Boheme*."

But I figured that I should revisit it, as a way of closing off, as a way of making sure I wasn't still doing it past forty. And what was really interesting—and this was not something we set out to do—was that, if you compare the production we did in 1990 with the 2003 one, the old one was a coarser show. But what's true about it is that it had a sort of brash youthfulness. It was all about the possibility of life and energy and saying, "Wow, isn't life going to be incredible?"

Now, having done it again, having turned forty-one and having just had a baby in the last few weeks—a little girl, Lillian—I think this production is a finer work. It's also more melancholic. It's not about lamenting the passing of that youth in the sense that "life will never be good again." It's about the naiveté of the ideals in the first place. An understanding that while those ideals are very real, the way in which one maintains an open heart, or a belief, or a search for some sort of truth, is not by keeping all the doors open. It's not by being extreme. It's not by going, "I'd rather die than . . ." Because you're just going to end up dying anyway.

We all know our friends from our bohemian youth and there were three kinds. There were those who actually did die of a drug overdose. There are those who actually stayed there mentally, and they are very sad. You just can't get through to them that it's time to grow up. And there are those who grew up. And, of the grown-up ones, there are those who get angry for some reason and say, "Oh, I was an idiot and I got ripped off by the commune," or whatever it was, "and you owe me money." But there are also those who are in the category that I hope stories like *La Boheme* can help with, and they say, "It was beautiful, it was extraordinary, it was exquisite, it was naïve, and it was perfect. But it could only be for a certain amount of time."

You can't explain this to a young person, but in trying to keep all the doors open, you're actually imprisoned by them. You're super-imprisoned by them. But when you close them, you're ready to begin the next journey, which isn't a physical one but a sort of spiritual one.

TK: In terms of the staging, what differences are there between Sydney and now?

BL: Well, Sydney itself was a very low-budget, tiny work. And it was part of a rep, remember, so it had to go in and out of the theater each night. The fundamental idea of the production, the heart of the idea of it, is very much the same. But in terms of the execution, now we're on a multi-million-dollar budget. And whereas the audience that was young and new to opera in Sydney were coming to the Opera House, now, we're going out to meet them half-way. We're going out into the jungle and we're saying, "Even if you've never seen an opera before, not only will you get the story, but you'll get everything and you'll be moved by it." It's a lot more lavish which enabled us to be very pictorially clear, to make it clear that you're on the streets of Paris in the fifties.

TK: Is it true that, when it was announced you were doing *La Boheme* in Sydney, nine-tenths of the subscribers cancelled?
BL: It happened. It was so weird. We were kids. I had my opera company, under the state opera company—it was experimental and we made operas—and I had my theater company. So I was one of those sort of irritating, young theater dynamos that made everyone go, "I want you dead. How can you be twenty-five and have two companies?" [laughs] But hey, it was a small town.

Then the chance to do *La Boheme* came along, and it was a big risk. We were only, like, twenty-three, twenty-four. So I spent like a year researching Puccini. The key thing for us was that it wasn't about reproducing the opera exactly, as they used to do in the 1800s. It was about recapturing what it felt like to be sitting in an audience in 1890, watching a show that was shocking: young middle-class guys hanging out with prostitutes, basically, living the bohemian life and dining on coffee.

It was very hard to communicate to a new audience that checked velvet pants and britches were shocking. So the choices were all based on how to make it feel like that experience. When our show was announced, there were virtually demonstrations from the opera lovers. On the week we opened, the Gulf War broke out. I can remember George Bush going, "We've got a war with Iraq," and we were doing *La Boheme*.

I noticed that, in the letter section of the *Sydney Morning Herald*, there were more letters saying, "We've got to stop these kids from doing *La Boheme*," than there were about what was going on in Iraq. What's slightly disturbing is that over ten years later, George Bush Jr. is still in Iraq and I'm still doing *La Boheme*. [laughs] I'd better stop doing it or we're really going to get into trouble, you know? So, yes indeed, the subscription cancellations happened. There were two big issues in this. One is that Joan Sutherland is really like our royalty. She's like the Queen in Australia. She was very negative about updating in general. We got the word: "Joan's not happy." So the Opera now was really out on a limb. I then learned to do what I'm doing now, to publicize. I learned that if you're going to take risks, you really need to get out there and explain it. I got on the chat shows. I had punk hair at the time—I've always had wacky hair—and that helped. I got the opportunity to state my case.

Then young people started to buy tickets and this became a big story. Sort of "Old is out, young is in." There weren't that many of them, but they started to line up and buy tickets. The next thing, we had Opening Night, and it was a great performance. People really rose to their feet, led by Joan Sutherland. Showing incredible grace, she came backstage and embraced us and told us how much she loved it. It went on to become their highest-grossing opera of all time. And the subscribers came back.

TK: What were some of the biggest challenges of doing the show on Broadway?
BL: Number one, above all else, was that, in Sydney, we cast this one young boy and one young girl in the leads. And now we needed three sets of leads. Not only did they all have to be truly able to sing it, but they had to look and act like their roles. So we did, like, a year of auditioning all over the world. I can't remember the numbers, but I did at least two hundred to three hundred all over the world. We chose one from Shanghai, one from Russia, one from America. It's the United Colors of Opera Singers, you know? They are all legitimate young stars and it's a real circus. They're brilliant young kids.

It's a beautiful thing, actually, and it was really only after we got going that people really realized how special it is. When you're young, there aren't that many young people around opera houses. So you've got these good-looking, young, groovy kids who equally like Radiohead and Puccini. On Broadway, there were fans looking for them. It was very cool.

TK: How did the decision to mike the performers come about? That's not traditional in the opera.
BL: Big, big decision. Because, you see, those kids can sing it any day you like. We'll come in and turn the sound system off and they'll still fill the room. The difference is that, when you're sitting in La Scala, or one of the other old houses, you can sit in the cheapest student seat, and, acoustically, it's immediate. It's not like that in the big houses on Broadway or here. So what the boys at Acme Sound have done—and we've spent a fortune getting this right—is not so much amplify the voice as change the acoustics of the space. So that if you're in a cheap seat, it feels resonant. It's not like a rock sound, where it's blaring out of a speaker

near your left ear. In fact, I have a rule: if they can spot where the sound is coming from, we're in trouble. So it's about it feeling resonant and sort of feeling liquid in the space.

TK: Is the show different from night to night, because you have such a diverse cast who rotate in the lead roles?

BL: Totally. But it delivers. People have their personal emotional connections to the performers. So it doesn't matter who it is. Someone will say, "I saw Wei Huang," and someone else will say, "Well, I saw Ekaterina." And you can't argue with them about who's better. But the truth is that what mostly happens is that people who have seen the show on more than one night have said, "I really enjoyed it because of the nuances in the differences of the performances." So it's a different nuance, not a different story.

TK: So is the Red Curtain kind of closing now, and are you going to move on to a new act in your filmmaking journey?

BL: Well, the curtain's come down on Act One on my life. These are undeniable things. Like we don't have endless acts in our lives, not yet. I think we might become really unfortunate if we do [laughs]. I have no doubt that in my lifetime, and yours, we're going to discover another twenty years. They're going to go, "Guess what. You've got another twenty years!" and we're going to go, "What do we do now?" Take another holiday, I suppose [laughs]. So, the first act is closed. I've turned forty, I had a little baby, and you go, "Life's fresh and new again. Act Two!"

I mean, I could make a living out of doing funky musicals. I sort of invented some of that language, so I could go on and do that forever. But I've made a choice that it's not about being the richest practitioner of what I do, or even the most famous, but about making sure that what we make is truly educating me and making my life just a rich one to live. Just a few weeks ago, working on *Alexander the Great*, I was in the jungles near the Burmese border with a bunch of elephants. I mean, how good does it get, you know? [laughs]

TK: How is your *Alexander the Great* project going?

BL: I've been working on the screenplay with David Hare. I'm basically back six months now because I need to give the screenplay another round. That's me, I take forever to do stuff. And Oliver Stone's doing his own version of the Alexander story, so everyone's happy I'm out of the way. And I have other epics too. The first way I get into trouble is that I talk about what I'm doing. Once I know what I'm going to do, I talk about it. But when I do it is up to me. We don't work for anyone else really.

TK: Have you settled on a style for the film yet?
BL: Its DNA is going to belong more to *Lawrence of Arabia* than to musical language. Its DNA comes from quite classical storytelling, quite classical cinema. But with an edge I guess. Although "edge" is a tricky word, because it's like [disdainfully] "let's make it edgy," you know? In the end, you shouldn't be starting at style. You should be making stylistic choices that help the audience experience and feel the story in this time and in this place. Stories do not change, but the way we tell them does.

* There is a DVD film of the 1993 production of Luhrmann's *La Boheme* at the Sydney Opera house available, directed for the Australian Broadcasting Commission by Geoffrey Nottage.

Australia: Baz Luhrmann Interview

Rob Carnevale / 2008

From IndieLondon (www.indielondon.co.uk), 2008. Reprinted by permission of the author.

Baz Luhrmann talks about the epic lengths he went to in order to realize his sweeping romantic drama, *Australia*, as well as about the significance of the historical events it depicts.

Rob Carnevale: Where did you get the inspiration for *Australia* and the style in which you told it?

Baz Luhrmann: Well, there's two parts to that. First, there's a childhood love of the genre, which involved me going back to my childhood and this cinematic banquet where you can have broad comedy, romance, action, and drama . . . all in one film. Those films, which I came into contact with when I was very, very young, made a great impression on me. Then you need to jump forward to a time when we were trying to make *Alexander the Great*. That was a great journey . . . I was working with the legendary Dino Di Laurentiis and Steven Spielberg. We built a studio in the Northern Sahara and Leonardo DiCaprio was set to star. It was an emotionally involving journey, but the film never happened because there was a competing project. But then Catherine Martin and I had another project in mind, which was to have our children. And we did a lot of work on that and had children!

We were living in Paris and I remember asking "Who are they?" Which, of course, is something a father should never ask [laughs, realizing what he has just said]. Or rather: "Where are they from?" We move in circles where you meet kids who say, "We spent three years in LA, and then a few years in Paris, etc., etc." But having roots seemed to be an extremely important thing. And that was the beginning of another journey that took us back to Australia four years ago. So I combined this personal journey with this love of the sweeping romantic epic.

Now, the films of the past that I spent my childhood with were invariably played out on an epic canvas of historical events and landscape. And, pretty quickly, it occurred to me that the historical event of the bombing of Darwin would be a good action sequence—plus it wasn't very well known, plus it was the same Japanese attack force that hit Pearl Harbor.

But the stolen generation stopped me in my tracks. I knew about it, but the more I researched it, the more I realized that this dark chapter was a scar on the story of our country. And that I was in a place where I could take something very serious and difficult—a difficult pill—and put it inside a great big entertainment.

This was the genesis of the idea. This was what made it more than a movie, because my children were going to grow up in an Australia where this stolen generation thing had never really been dealt with. It had in smaller films, but not in a way which would mean it could never be swept under the carpet. So I felt I could do that and, foolishly perhaps, combined those two things. So, that was day one, four years ago. . . .

RC: And the journey isn't yet complete. You only just finished the film. . . .

BL: It's so crazy because three weeks ago I was literally at a mixing desk doing the final voiceover, and recording little Nullah (Brandon Walters). . . . The truth is, you never finish movies—they just get taken away from you! That was a Friday, and the following Tuesday some three thousand people saw it in one sitting in Sydney. We got on the plane the next day, went to Los Angeles and did a junket there, then to New York, and this week we've been in Paris, Madrid, and Rome . . . and now we're here [in London]. And I still haven't finished. But that's sort of the way it is with me. . . . None of my films are really finished. They've crossed the line and sort of lived.

RC: How much research did you do?

BL: Well, there's this thing called research which is fun and obsessive and relentless, so every image ever printed from that period we would have collected. Everything comes from the research and reality . . . but then again, the film is a romance, so it's an interpretation. We had a rule, which was: so long as it doesn't fundamentally change the truth, we could make a conjuncture. I had a lot of start-up images, but my first dialogue is always with Catherine, where we create the visual language. She then goes out and talks to hundreds of other people.

We then create the books, which start with the written script and the visual script. It is a book per scene . . . so if the scene's set at the homestead, it'll include all the different images of a homestead. Then that book, through photo-shop work, is turned into characterizations in those locations. For the drawings, we work with lots of artists. Eventually, once Hugh [Jackman] comes on to the production, we start fittings and photo-shop him into the book. And then, when we finish making the final movie, we make the final book, because in the end it's storytelling—and it becomes a storytelling book with pictures.

RC: Nicole Kidman has been quoted as saying there'll never be an Australian movie like this again. And yet you've said you conceived this as part of a trilogy. So, who is right?

BL: I think she meant something different. I think what she's saying first of all has to do with the cast, the serendipitous nature of how it came together. . . . I'd like to think that a film like this could be made again and that there will be more films made like this, of this scale, that are Australian stories with Australian practitioners . . . doing what America has done for a very long time, which is to take their storytelling on to a level that will play around the globe.

I think what Nicole might be getting at, though, and this is probably right, is that to go out into the landscape with two hundred crew members in put-up tents, and actually go out there and shoot on location is an approach to production that is definitely dying. We barely got away with it. We mixed the Lean, which is shooting on location, with the Lucas, which is using visual effects. Maybe it will happen again. But I know what Nicole means is that, for a variety of reasons, it will certainly never happen in this manner again.

As for the trilogy: yes, I was a fool to say I was doing three epics because one nearly killed me. But I do have them. I have a room full of things I want to make before I'm shuffled off this mortal coil, and they're in a variety of sizes. The only thing I will say is that, once I work out what's worth doing next, don't be surprised if it's something fun and quick before I get on to do the next major work because they just take a lot of time.

RC: Do you think there should be more gratuitous torso shots in Hollywood movies?

BL: It's actually a much more serious question that you think [laughs]. It is much harder for actors, particularly in cinema, to do that sort of broad humor. I'm not saying anything less about exploring the emotional depths . . . but you expect that in the current cinematic vernacular. So, to have Hugh and Nicole go out and take on so many different genres . . . the requisite bravery in doing that is far more petrifying, and a much bigger ask, than asking them to do the dramatic, sweeping epic stuff.

RC: Did you fall in love with Brandon Walters, your Nullah, because of his eyes?

BL: Yes. If there's an incredible thing in this movie, it is that boy. To give you some context . . . as I speak to you, he's probably hitting some creature on the head with a lump of wood in the bush. But it was bold to say, "Let's have a seven-year-old Aboriginal boy be the co-lead in the film!" I would have trouble finding a European boy of that age who could act. So, to find that boy was a living nightmare. The team saw a thousand boys to start with. That little fella was incredible. He's actually not acting. Something real is just so much more affecting. The truth is: he doesn't read the camera. He looks past it with the eyes. So did I fall in love with his eyes? Yes, because his eyes don't play for the camera. He was quite a miracle and we were lucky to have him because no Brandon, no movie.

RC: I'm assuming that filming with the likes of Bryan Brown and Jack Thompson had its fair share of moments?

BL: I kind of imagine it was the equivalent of the days of working with Richard Harris and Peter O'Toole, just in a different style. When I was a kid, I acted in a film with Bryan Brown and he was an absolute icon. And Jack had two wives, who were sisters. . . . Which, given that it's illegal in our country, is a hell of an achievement! He was also an absolute sex god, like the Brad Pitt of our time. So, to think that one day I'd do a film in which there was a little Aboriginal boy, the current reigning Australian actors in the world, Hugh and Nicole, David Gulpilil—remember *Walkabout?*—and then Bryan and Jack. . . . I'm privileged. Imagine what it was like for me? The guys I grew up with, my contemporaries, and the upcoming generation . . . so maybe that's another part of what Nicole meant. Maybe that's what won't happen again.

Did you also know that Jack began his life as a ringer on a cattle station, and was fired for being too friendly with the Aboriginal stockmen? So, can you imagine when I pitched the film to him. He said, "This is my life. . . ."

Strictly Luhrmann: Where He Leads, We Will Follow

James Mottram / 2010

From the *Independent*, October 22, 2010. Reprinted by permission of the author.

A gloomy autumn day in New York, and the weather has already left its mark on Baz Luhrmann. "It's a bit miserable today," he sighs. "Up until now it's been gorgeous." As are the films of the Australian director, with their rich, multi-colored palettes exploding from the screen; it's little wonder today's grey Manhattan skies do little for him. Bold and brash, the flamboyant Luhrmann doesn't so much see the world through rose-tinted spectacles, as through rainbow-colored ones.

The forty-eight-year-old is in town to present scenes from the forth-coming Blu-ray editions of two of his most colorful films: 1996's Shake-speare reboot, *Romeo + Juliet*, and 2001's musical *Moulin Rouge!* Revisit-ing them has been educational, he says. "It's probably the first time that I've actually seen them as films, if that makes sense. I'm old enough and distant enough now to not just see them as troubling but much-loved children; they've grown up, and got relationships with audiences that have nothing to do with me."

Fans of the films will obviously be lured by the fact that Luhrmann has dipped into the vaults of his company, Bazmark, to pull out some never-before-seen footage for the accompanying extras. Highlights in-clude Nicole Kidman's first vocal test on *Moulin Rouge!* and the first on-camera kiss between *Romeo + Juliet* stars Leonardo DiCaprio and Claire Danes. "It was basically a costume test," explains the director. "It's quite wonderful to see Leonardo so caring for Claire, and how really beautiful it is. It's just a very beautiful moment."

Yet, more importantly, the films act as a reminder of just how pre-scient Luhrmann is as a director. Together with their predecessor, his 1992 directorial debut, *Strictly Ballroom*, outside of the original *Star Wars* trilogy, you'd be hard pressed to find a trio of movies more influential on popular culture right now. Without *Strictly Ballroom*, there'd be no

Strictly Come Dancing. Without *Moulin Rouge!*, there'd be no *Glee.* And without *Romeo + Juliet*, there'd be no *10 Things I Hate About You* or any of the other Shakespeare adaptations aimed at adolescents.

Indeed, living in the US right now, Luhrmann can't escape his own influence. Currently in its second season, the Golden Globe–winning *Glee* is "the biggest show in America," he claims. A high-school tale, in which the characters burst into well-known show-tunes and pop songs, its style is one Luhrmann popularized in *Moulin Rouge!* "[*Glee* co-creator] Ryan Murphy has been very nice about acknowledging that it was *Moulin Rouge!* that inspired him," says Luhrmann. "But ten years ago . . . if I had a dollar for everyone that said, 'The musical will never be popular in America.' . . ."

The same goes for *Strictly Ballroom*, a film based on his own experiences in the world of ballroom dancing as a youngster. "Executives would say, 'Ballroom dancing will never be popular in America.' It's crazy. I turn on CNN and the headline is 'Trouble in Afghanistan' followed by 'And the Hoff has been thrown out of *Dancing with the Stars.*'"

As if to signify his contribution to what has become a cultural phenomenon around the globe, producers of this US version of the celebrity dance show even invited Luhrmann on as a guest judge, to explain to the audience that the BBC original was "directly inspired" by his own film.

As for *Romeo + Juliet*, Luhrmann is justifiably proud that the film, be it due to the sexy casting of DiCaprio and Danes as Shakespeare's star-crossed lovers or the MTV-style visuals, influenced a generation of teenagers. "I've had people from the education system come up and say that has been their major instrument in re-engaging young audiences in Shakespeare." Such is the film's impact almost a decade and a half on, says Luhrmann, "sometimes teachers tell me they have a very hard time convincing students that Romeo and Juliet didn't meet each other in a swimming pool in the original text!"

Luhrmann shrugs at the notion that everything he touches turns to gold, reminding me that back then people were "outraged" by his approach to Shakespeare (even though he'd already successfully staged a colonial India-set version of *A Midsummer's Night's Dream* back in 1993). "In terms of *Romeo + Juliet, Strictly Ballroom,* and *Moulin Rouge!*, what made them so controversial ten years ago . . . it's not even a headline now. What's different is that they've had such a connection to the culture that now people are really interested to revisit them as adults."

While the three films were dubbed Luhrmann's "red curtain trilogy," he maintains that the theatrical philosophy (simple story, heightened

reality) behind them was inspired by what informed him growing up—
"a love of classic cinema." Raised in Herons Creek, a rural town in New
South Wales, Luhrmann says his film tastes were fostered by his ex–Navy
Seal father, who ran a local movie theater. Among his earliest memo-
ries are watching his father thread up films in the projection room and
watching the theater's plush red curtain draw back to screen such Hollywood musicals as *The Sound of Music* and *Paint Your Wagon*.

Yet, curiously, while the world latched on to Luhrmann's "red-
curtain" aesthetic, the director turned his back on it and aimed for "a
more epic style." First there was his aborted project about Alexander
the Great, partially abandoned, he says, because he didn't want to get
into "a Hollywood race" with Oliver Stone, who eventually released a
much-maligned version starring Colin Farrell. Then came *Australia*, a
reunion with Nicole Kidman that proved his Midas touch was not infal-
lible. Luhrmann's bloated epic romance is set in the country during the
build-up to the Second World War and it's hard to imagine it influencing
popular culture in the way its predecessors have.

Two years on from that disappointment, Luhrmann claims he is just
"six weeks away" from deciding what his next film will be. The smart
money is on another epic, an adaptation of F. Scott Fitzgerald's *The Great
Gatsby*, which was previously brought to the screen in the disappoint-
ing 1974 version starring Robert Redford. "It's second only to *Gone with
the Wind* as a recognizable title," says Luhrmann, "and what defines it is
that it captures something absolutely inherent to the American condition. Gatsby is born with ambition and possibility. And when that meets
opportunity, it can be both beautiful and tragic in an operatic sense."

He concedes that—much like he did with the boldly named *Australia*—he's setting himself up for a fall by tackling such a title. "I don't really care about that. I go towards things that are challenging for me and
scary for me—but I want to see them up there. If I'd walked away from
that, I wouldn't have tried to reinvent the musical, or had a go at making
Shakespeare popular, or done a ballroom dancing film. Nobody turns
around and goes 'Yes, ballroom dancing, definitely! We want that!'"

Maybe that was true when he started *Strictly Ballroom*, but not anymore. While he considers his next film, Luhrmann is now planning a
stage-musical version of the film, which he intends to start working on
when he returns to Sydney in December. "I think the thing I'm going to
be attending to with the production is keeping the familiar elements—
that is plot and characters and sensibility. But I'll also look at the underlying myth of oppression, whether that's artistic or political. This

idea that there's a big powerful federation with a special, private magical book that tells you there's only one way to cha-cha-cha . . . I'd really like to address that."

In some ways, it will bring Luhrmann full circle, given that *Strictly Ballroom* began life in 1986 as a twenty-minute play he created while studying at the National Institute of Dramatic Art in Sydney (it later doubled in length and was taken to the World Youth Theater Festival in a "pre-glasnost Czechoslovakia"). While the film itself was the play's next stage of evolution, it's now set to return to its roots. "Maybe its execution will be wildly simple," Luhrmann suggests. "I'm going in with a very open heart and mind as to how to represent it in a way in which it's both familiar but also pushing the boundaries in terms of music theater."

Given the recent successes of other film-to-stage adaptations, such as *Dirty Dancing* and *Grease*, it's what you might call a no-brainer. One can only hope that, when it comes to publicizing it, Luhrmann takes a slot on *Strictly Come Dancing*. Would he ever consider it? He lets out a machine-gun laugh. "I have been asked! And I love to dance. I really do love to dance. But, no . . . I've got so many day jobs." He stops and chews the idea over for a second. "Maybe in my dotage. 'Here he comes now—he's got the walker!'" It's a delicious image: the man behind the red curtain finally stepping out to show us his cha-cha-cha.

The Romantic

Garry Maddox / 2013

Originally published in *Good Weekend Magazine* in the *Sydney Morning Herald* and *The Age*, May 11, 2013. Reprinted by permission of the author.

The day starts with breakfast at Tiffany's. With the world premiere of *The Great Gatsby* looming, Baz Luhrmann is telling an early-morning audience at the New York jewellers how he was captivated by F. Scott Fitzgerald's classic novel on, of all places, the Trans-Siberian Express. Having planned what he thought was a luxurious train journey to unwind after *Moulin Rouge!* (it turned out to be the railway equivalent of a tin box), he listened at night to an audio version on his iPod, with two bottles of Australian red as his only company. Scrambling to remember the year, the dapper director jokes that numbers aren't his strong point: "Ask the studio."

Seated beside his creative partner and wife Catherine Martin at the launch of Tiffany's *Gatsby*-themed window displays, Luhrmann says he was so captivated by the novel that "at the end of it, I went, 'There's a movie here I have to make.'" The audience is absorbed, as it generally is when the director of *Strictly Ballroom* (1992), *Romeo + Juliet* (1996), *Moulin Rouge!* (2001), and *Australia* (2008) has the floor.

It is easy to see why so many people, even in hard-headed Hollywood, say yes to him as they listen to a passionate volley of words, ideas, and images, underscored by flamboyant gestures that bring a planned movie to life. He charms with jokey impressions that often drop important names: Marlon Brando writing to ask for a role in *Romeo + Juliet*, for example. Then, as at Tiffany's, Luhrmann will often conjure up a touching story about growing up in the small town of Herons Creek on the NSW north coast, where his father ran a service station and later a cinema.

This is the public side of a filmmaker who, at fifty, has gone from that hamlet of just eleven houses to co-writing, directing, and producing one of the highest-profile movies this year, a sumptuous drama about a gilded millionaire, Jay Gatsby, pining for the love of his life, Daisy Buchanan.

For *The Great Gatsby*, Luhrmann brought together some of the biggest names—brands if you like—in global entertainment and fashion: Leonardo DiCaprio as Gatsby, hip-hop star Jay-Z as music and executive producer, Tiffany's, Prada, and Brooks Brothers to collaborate with Martin on designs, with songs by Beyoncé, Florence Welch, Gotye, and Jack White. All have gambled their time and reputation on a risky 3D drama estimated to cost more than $180 million, including Australian federal and state government subsidies of at least $80 million. *Gatsby* is a New York story, set in the roaring twenties, which Luhrmann wanted to shoot in Sydney. It's also a literary adaptation that, after delays for rain and his obsessive desire to elaborate, finesse, and perfect, is competing with such American summer blockbusters as *Iron Man 3* and *Star Trek Into Darkness*.

Luhrmann talked his first film into reality in 1990. When a commissioned script for *Strictly Ballroom* wasn't working—it had started life as a stage version devised with his fellow students at the National Institute of Dramatic Art—producer Tristram Miall suggested he just tell them the story. So he did, playing all the parts.

"We put on a tape recorder and Baz told the story of this young prince of the ballroom world who wanted to dance his own steps," Miall says. "He got up and danced around and he basically did a Baz. He conjures up fabulous images. And we said, 'Yeah, that's it. Just go away and write it.'"

He has become one of the country's leading filmmakers, but while Peter Weir and Jane Campion are revered, Luhrmann attracts more than his share of criticism. Some of it comes from reviewers, who consider his films overwrought and over-hyped, some from other filmmakers, who grimace at the way his ambitious productions haemorrhage money and exhaust crews, and some from gossip columnists, who see him, being famous, as fair game.

But even his harshest critics would agree that Luhrmann's creative record is as rich as his *Moulin Rouge!* nightclub scenes. While *Australia* disappointed at the US box office and was sometimes savagely reviewed, it did strong business in other parts of the world. He has also directed memorable opera productions of *La Bohème* and *A Midsummer Night's Dream* for the stage and produced mega-selling soundtracks. He has shot commercials for Chanel No. 5 and, just recently, a series of short films with Prada executive Miuccia Prada. He is developing a stage musical of *Strictly Ballroom* and a television series for Sony.

Struck by Paul Keating's big-picture views on Australia's place in the world and on indigenous Australia, he helped Labor during the 1993 federal election campaign—including "styling and image representation" and staging the campaign launch. He even designed a kitschy Australian theme park with Martin and fellow director Barrie Kosky, the Fox Studios Backlot at Sydney's Moore Park.

He has had failures. When Oliver Stone got in first, he had to abandon plans for his Alexander the Great movie. The Fox Backlot never struck a chord. Sony backed out of *Gatsby* because it was too expensive before Warner Bros. stepped in. But Luhrmann inhabits a surreal world where, as well as turning down James Bond and Harry Potter movies, he once fielded an offer to rebrand a religion, though he won't say which one.

Carey Mulligan, who plays Gatsby's great love Daisy Buchanan, says, "Baz is like director/host/uncle. He does everything and he does it with such grace." Joel Edgerton, who plays her brutish husband Tom, calls him "a perfect director" who always seems to have time for actors. "I've never seen him lose his temper," he says.

And when it comes to persuasion, Luhrmann is as effective as Lionel Messi is with a football at his feet. "I don't think *Moulin Rouge!* deserved to do the business it did," says an Australian filmmaker, speaking anonymously. "It was a pretty indifferent story. But he got out and sold it."

Martin Brown, who produced that film, says Luhrmann talks for a living, in a way. "He's always convincing, always persuading, always cajoling, always bludgeoning when required, always getting people to do what he wants."

The day finishes with a second trip to Tiffany's, for a cocktail party that could have been thrown by Gatsby himself. Waiters serve champagne and JG-monogrammed canapés while guests circle glass cabinets studying jewellery from the movie. Luhrmann greets people with warm hugs, has his photo taken, tells a story about chasing down a first edition of *The Great Gatsby* to send to DiCaprio ("My assistant called and said, 'Are you sure you want to do this? It costs half a million dollars.' I said, 'Ah, is there one for, say, five thousand dollars?'"), counsels a young filmmaker, and has his photo taken again.

The private Baz Luhrmann is quieter, more thoughtful, and wracked with doubt. "Sometimes, I admit, I must be maddening," he says. "There are so many mad systems I've got around me, just to keep me moving through time and space, because my mind is always on."

Dressed down stylishly in a red T-shirt, tailored blue pants, and blue slip-ons without socks, the unshaven, silver-haired Luhrmann is at home in Greenwich Village. To get to his office/studio on the top floor, you walk up three flights of stairs, past Catherine Martin—designer and his first sounding board on every creative project for more than twenty-five years—who breaks from her computer on the third floor to say hello.

If this is a sanctuary, an open and sunny room with a double bed tucked in one corner, it is a busy one, with people coming and going regularly. Even when he seems relaxed, Luhrmann's mind is darting in different directions. He tugs nervously at one sleeve of his T-shirt at one point. Later, he strokes his forearm like it's a cat.

The house cook, who has arrived breathless after walking up from the ground floor, wants a lunch order. Luhrmann goes for soup—"in the middle of the day, I'm just so churned up"—before inquiring about "some sort of wrap with amazing tahini stuff" that he loved the day before.

"I could have been eating venison and squab, it was so delicious," he says to the cook in a manic burst of words. "I was crazy for it. And before the ball tonight, can you find out if it's a sit-down in terms of dinner or do we dine before we go? If it's sit-down, can you find out if they're serving fish or whatever? And maybe a little hit of protein just before we go." One of two young, casually dressed assistants, Blakey, is dispatched to fix an audio problem and sort out clothes and other preparations for the ball.

When the couple are in New York, they live in this Greenwich Village house with their two children, Lilly, nine, and Will, seven. Their Sydney home is Iona, a grand Darlinghurst mansion behind an iron gate with a handsome verandah and rolling lawn. They bought it for $A10 million in 2006 after renting it as both their residence and the offices of their production company, Bazmark, for almost a decade. During busy times it is a frantic tangle of people working on designs and planning productions, while the family lives upstairs.

They have listed Iona—for $A15 million—so that they can move to a house closer to the water and run a separate studio. Luhrmann was upset by a story in Sydney's *Sunday Telegraph* that he says wrongly claimed they were being forced to sell because of budget over-runs on *Gatsby*.

Their Greenwich Village house is much more down-to-earth than Iona: nothing special outside, modern and friendly inside. But just over a fortnight before the premiere, it is the center of hundreds of small jobs to launch *Gatsby*.

"I exhaust people so much," Luhrmann says, resigned to it. "We have these Bazmark rules: I recognize [my team] need to sleep odd and weird hours because we just work . . . well, it's a blur." When things get too much, anyone can take "a NASA nap: no less than twenty minutes, no more than forty."

Luhrmann is not a napper, though. His racing mind won't slow down enough. "I'm an incredibly difficult sleeper," he says. "I can have periods when I really believe [the night] will never end and I'm dancing with devils and demons. It's terrifying and I just can't wait for the sun to come up."

"It's a whacky thing, my sleep. It's imagination-related. I've got the basic things like everyone has: 'My god, I've got some big deal tomorrow.' But a lot of it is like fighting—not verbal fighting, it's emotional fighting. I've got to find within myself the confidence or the belief to convey an idea."

So how many hours does he sleep? "I won't name the drugs, but let's say I'll take a sleeping potion. But even with that, I always sleep for about four hours, then I wake up and I have to go back for another bout. When I actually have REM, it's like I've visited some exotic island and gone, 'Oh my God, I remember what it's like to have a holiday.'"

Blakey apologetically interrupts with a "time-sensitive question" about dressing for the ball, given that Prada's tailored shirts won't be ready in time. Does he want Tiffany's to give him some studs? "Stud me up," Luhrmann says, as precise about clothes as he is about food and what he wants in his movies. "I'd like to wear the JG green cuff links from the Jay Gatsby range and I'll wear as much bling as they want. Ring Prada and get the shirts off the rack that fit me."

Dressing appropriately is part of the job. "I want people to feel comfortable and I want to relate to them," Luhrmann says. "On *Gatsby*, I wore shorts for the first time. I saw Wim Wenders once wearing shorts and I thought, 'God, how can you direct in shorts?' I tried it one day. It was only second unit [rather than the main filming unit], so it was kind of fun. But you can't direct in shorts. You're actually leading an army."

Dotted around the walls of his office are giant Post-it notes listing important dates, jobs to be done, scenes in scripts, people to talk to, meetings required, and cryptic notes like "Snap to black slow motion silhouettes—Ballroom couples prepare" and "5.00–6.00 Prep for Blue Book Ball." Dates crossed off a calendar show the countdown to "New York premiere," "Anna dinner," "Met ball," "Film opens USA," and "Cannes Premiere."

"I've spent my life surrounded by crazy lists and charts," Luhrmann says. "I think I've constructed a way, my way, of getting what's inside my head out. I write my own writing but I can't read it. No one can read my writing. See these funny little notebooks"—he points to two leather-bound books on the table—"they're everywhere. [In] that one I've made an effort to write clearly, so I must have been really worried. But I've got notebooks that are just mad scrawls and squiggles."

Another system is having "rollers" everywhere—dictaphones—so he can compose notes on creative projects, thank-you letters, messages to corporate types, things to do, or just ideas to be typed up by his team, even when he is supposed to be relaxing with a massage. Blakey lays out notebooks and writing boards at night, then collects them in the morning to keep on top of ideas and things needing to be done.

While he tends to forget his keys—one hangs around his neck now after he had to wake Martin to get into the house the previous night—Luhrmann has a near-photographic memory for film takes and music tracks. "If I've shot something and thought, 'That's going to work,' I never forget it," he says. But his memory has limits. "A lot of people remember very intense things they've been through with me. But I don't remember the intense things I've been through with them that might be negative. It's a big deal for them, but less so for me because I'm down the road on the next thing."

Creativity, he says, is about facing your fears. And his fears include just about everything. "I deal with them usually in the first twenty minutes when I get up in the morning. Spit 'em all out. When I'm in the moment, I just can't afford fear. I have [fears] and I have them every day. But when I go into my job, I have to flick the switch to action."

Pressed on those fears, Luhrmann rattles through a rapid-fire list. "Is it going to be on time? What was I thinking? Why *The Great Gatsby*? What an idiot! Can't I just do something small? I thought *The Great Gatsby* would be a simple, small project. It was essentially going to be acting in rooms. Then I started my journey and realized Fitzgerald loved modernism, he loved cinema. Jim Cameron had shown me very early on the testings he was doing for *Avatar*. I thought, '3D is a drama.' I saw *Dial M for Murder* and went, 'Well, 3D is just a little bit of [extra] expense.'"

He continues with hardly a breath taken. "I thought Leonardo DiCaprio must be Jay Gatsby. Jay-Z would be great for the music. My old friend Miuccia Prada will collaborate. And, of course, one has always got to remember that a real genius like Fitzgerald would be able to make a compact novella, but what it really is is a massive compression of epic emotions and epic physical locations into what seems a slender novella. When you go in to make it cinematic, somehow it grows."

But where does all this restless creativity come from? "I've always done what I do right now," he says. "You know why I can articulate that: I see it in my son. Will is constantly in his own world at a very intense level. He says, 'I need to be in my own world for a moment, Dad.' I was like that with a father who was very disciplined yet very driven, and a creative and very theatrical mother who saw things through a romantic lens."

According to one friend, when the young Luhrmann boys were handed tea towels to help with washing up, Baz would turn his into a cape or a theatrical costume: "Not so much drying up happened, but quite a lot of theatricality."

Martin, who met Luhrmann at an interview for a Bicentennial opera project in 1987, says his family remember him as a great storyteller, even as a child. "He has a desire to make things, like a conjurer, appear out of nothing, to make ethereal ideas a reality," she says. "We're both romantics—not in a Valentine's Day card kind of way, but in that eighteenth- and early nineteenth-century ideal of romanticism, where there's a love of the big idea and the adventure and making something that has meaning or beauty or expresses the human condition or celebrates it in some way."

Hence the upbeat ideas in the movies—"a life lived in fear is a life half-lived" from *Strictly Ballroom*; "the greatest thing you will ever learn is just to love and be loved in return" from *Moulin Rouge!*—as characters struggle with love, loss, and death.

Long-time writing partner Craig Pearce has been friends with Luhrmann since year eleven at Narrabeen High School, on Sydney's northern beaches, when they discovered they both wanted to be actors. The Luhrmann family had lived down the road until Baz's father, a former navy clearance diver who served in Vietnam, shifted the family—three sons with military-cropped hair and a daughter—to Herons Creek. When his parents divorced, Luhrmann stayed with his dad, then snuck away at twelve to live with his mother back at Narrabeen. "He was always different," says Pearce.

Mark Luhrmann reinvented himself by shortening his nickname, "Basil," which came from his Basil Brush hairstyle. "He always had this tremendous sense of destiny, this tremendous belief that he was going to create amazing things and do amazing things," Pearce says. "He's always had an incredible imagination and a desire to make life bigger and better and more exciting than it is."

Pearce sees another side to the public Luhrmann. "He gets depressed. He gets down. There're always really hard moments on any project. With *Australia*, even though it was ultimately successful at the box office, there were terrible, terrible reviews. I know he found that very hard." Luhrmann says he has spiralled half a dozen times into black despair after bitter disappointments.

The prescription, outside of spending time with his children, is often work. "Baz is able to work every waking second," says Martin Brown. "I don't think there's an off switch." But what about downtime? Surely the couple went to the beach or the football sometimes during the decade he worked with them? "There was no downtime," Brown says. "Never. Literally never."

It's day seventy-six on the set of *The Great Gatsby* at Sydney's Fox Studios. Luhrmann is directing a party scene on Gatsby's terrace that shows the vast scale of the production. DiCaprio, Tobey Maguire, and Elizabeth Debicki as Daisy's friend, Jordan Baker, are in the center of the huge sound stage, surrounded by 250 extras as stunningly dressed, made-up, coiffed, and bejeweled as the stars. A swimming pool has the same JG monogram on the bottom as will be found on the Tiffany's canapés some sixteen months later. "Off we go," shouts Luhrmann. Orchestral music swells, people dance, fireworks go off, the crowd screams.

"The whole thing is incredible," says Maguire, in character as Nick Carraway, astonished at the party's opulence and madness. "I live just next door. He sent me an invitation. Seems I'm the only one. I haven't met Mr. Gatsby. No one's met him. They say he's second cousin to the Kaiser and third cousin to the devil." DiCaprio chimes in, "I'm afraid I haven't been a very good host, old sport. You see, *I'm* Gatsby." Amid the chaos, Luhrmann wants the shot again. And again. And again.

But when the crew goes on location, they strike wet weather. Just as they did on *Romeo + Juliet*, when a hurricane forced them to relocate. And on *Australia*, when rain and an equine flu outbreak disrupted the schedule.

"If I have one gift, it's to attract extraordinary weather to places where it doesn't occur," he says in New York. "They should truly, honestly, think about using me to re-vegetate deserts. I just have to turn up and it rains. But probably the reason it does rain is that everything I'm trying to do is sort of unprecedented, it's sort of unpredictable."

As well as an injury to Luhrmann—filming had to shut down early before Christmas 2011 when he cut his head open on a camera crane—the director's perfectionism, the demands of 3D, and work on the music pushed back the *Gatsby* release date by five months. This is where another of Luhrmann's talents comes in, a knack for inspiring a crew through an exhausting shoot.

"He works in a way that's very personal," says a former crew member. "Men and women will say he's very seductive in a way. Both he and Catherine work hard at instilling a kind of religious fervor in what they do. On his projects, it's more like a cult than a crew. He has a messianic quality."

Luhrmann sees it another way: "If it's a cult, then I'm just an acolyte serving a force greater than all of us and that's the story," he says. And while he doesn't plan to be ambitious on set, he tends to think "what if?" a lot, which leads to the budget going up. Luhrmann says studios only think about one question: Is the number a good piece of business?

"When it comes to my work, even the idea of doing it isn't a good piece of business," he says. "It's madness. All the films I've made should never have got made. Anyone will tell you that." Not until, that is, the conjurer, the passionate enthusiast with the big ideas, talks them into reality.

Baz Luhrmann's Despair, Drive, and Gamble behind *Great Gatsby*

Stephen Galloway / 2013

From the *Hollywood Reporter*, April 24, 2013. Published with the permission of the *Hollywood Reporter*.

Like his protagonist Jay Gatsby, the Australian director once reinvented himself with a name change and new identity. Now, he's risked everything on his flashy $100 million spectacle: "I would do anything to make sure *Gatsby* stayed alive."

Seven years after he first had contemplated adapting F. Scott Fitzgerald's 1925 novel about obsessive love, the director's passion project was in trouble. New York, where he had hoped to shoot, was proving too expensive for Sony, which wanted to limit his budget to $80 million, and now the studio insisted on finding partners to defray the cost. Without them, the movie was dead.

So in January of that year, Luhrmann plunged into a Warner Bros. conference room, where he met such top-level executives as Jeff Robinov, Greg Silverman, Veronika Kwan Vandenberg, and Kevin Tsujihara. For two hours, he bewitched them with a torrent of words explaining how he would mix old and new, blend hip-hop with sounds from the twenties, and use 3D to make the movie modern—all while showing clips he'd videotaped of Leonardo DiCaprio workshopping scenes. "I went into that room and thought, 'In this moment, I've got to tell this story like I've never told it before,'" he recalls.

Sitting with the fifty-year-old Australian on a mid-April afternoon in New York's Ace Hotel, not far from the place he now calls home and in the very room where he and writing partner Craig Pearce wrote their script, it's easy to understand why Warners said yes. He virtually bubbles over with passion, his enthusiasm erupting in a cavalcade of words.

He can entrance you with tales of dining alongside Bill Clinton at his neighbor Anna Wintour's (he does a spot-on impersonation of the former president); or having David Bowie walk his dogs; or discussing 3D with Ang Lee and James Cameron. All this he does with such a lack of self-consciousness, you almost overlook the name-dropping—helped by his touch of Gatsby's flair, with his immaculately coiffed silver hair, Patek Philippe watch (a gift from Tiffany & Co., a marketing partner on the film), and gleaming shoes on sockless feet.

Sometimes manic, sometimes more modulated, he flits from one subject to another without pause—from the books he's been reading (Mikhail Bulgakov's *The Master and the Margarita* and Jay-Z's *Decoded*) to the TV shows he watches with his children (Disney's *Gravity Falls*, when not skipping among CNN, the BBC, and Fox) to his hair. Especially his hair.

"I've had it since I was thirty," he says, referring to its whiteness. "I'll be honest about that. I used to dye my hair on *Moulin Rouge!* My hair went half-gray on one side, and I thought, 'I am going to get ahead of the game.'"

He says this with an intensity that he maintains whether his subject is the mythological Pothos (a symbol of yearning) or the "babushka" who showed him a hose that doubled as a shower when he was once traveling on a Russian train. This and his ability to mix high and low are key to "Brand Baz," as he puts it, and have stamped his empire, Bazmark Inq., with divisions handling design, film, live entertainment, music, and housewares.

Running it keeps him constantly in motion, from the time he wakes (around 8:30 A.M. when he's not shooting) to the moment he goes to sleep (as late as 2:00 or 3:00 A.M.)—often staying in bed for chunks of the day as his collaborators shuffle around him. But strip away the sizzle and a rather different person emerges, both shyer and more vulnerable than the compulsive showman he sometimes appears to be.

This is the man who admits to self-doubt, speaks of bitter disappointments, and sporadic depressions; who says he was devastated when his Alexander the Great biopic crumbled after years of work and describes instances of a black despair that left him feeling almost suicidal—"very rarely, but when I do, it's totally real. It's been a half-dozen times, and it's deep."

This also is the man who occasionally questions his own work, no matter how much he might trumpet it in public: "I am always worried when someone says, 'This is perfect,'" he admits in a rare moment of introspection. "I have doubts; nothing is ever really good enough. Is it worthwhile? Is it of value?"

International audiences will decide that when Gatsby opens the Festival de Cannes on May 15, following its domestic release. After a protracted battle for the rights and a troubled shoot that eventually led the film to cost $104.5 million (it would have cost more than $190 million without hefty Australian location subsidies), the picture is being given a massive push by Warners, which is counting on its mix of star-laden cast, cutting-edge soundtrack (produced by Jay-Z), and period glamor to win over young audiences.

A Tiffany deal (the company designed jewelry for the film and has created its own *Great Gatsby* collection) and some lavish costumes by Luhrmann's friend Miuccia Prada are all elements in making this an event, perhaps *the* event of early summer.

That will be boosted by DiCaprio, who reteams with Luhrmann for the first time since 1996's *Romeo + Juliet*, giving young women another chance to see him in a love story—though the actor says Gatsby is far more nuanced than that.

"My recollection from high school was always of this hopeless romantic," says DiCaprio of the novel's title character, noting that Luhrmann gave him a first edition several years ago. "I didn't quite see the emptiness of Jay Gatsby. He concentrates on his love of this woman, but does he really love her? When he finally has her in his arms, is it enough and is she enough?"

The fact that DiCaprio had another film out late last year, *Django Unchained*, was one reason Warners pushed the Gatsby opening from Christmas to early summer. "Finishing the soundtrack and the visual effects and perfecting everything into 3D—Baz could have made the release date," says Robinov. "But we said, 'Give this enough time to make it great.'"

Greatness may have seemed a long way off during the Australian shoot, when one disaster followed another, culminating in a crane cracking open Luhrmann's head. "It was scary," says DiCaprio. "But he handled it like, 'Oh, it's just a bump!'—like Mercutio in *Romeo + Juliet*—'A scratch, a mere scratch. I would love to keep filming, but they tell me I must go to the hospital.' I have never seen anyone be able to keep going like that."

Born in 1962, Mark Anthony Luhrmann was a young child when his family relocated to the eleven-house hamlet of Herons Creek, where his father operated a gas station and movie theater in the shadow of a deadly bridge from which drivers occasionally would plummet to their deaths.

A Vietnam vet and reformed alcoholic, Leonard Luhrmann pushed his four kids relentlessly, rousing them at dawn, putting them through commando exercises and forcing his three boys to have military-style crew cuts. "Long hair defined the era," his son explains. "My brother suffered great physical violence, and it was all about the short hair. People would beat you up because you were weirdos."

Insisting on this was just one of his father's eccentricities. Once, "he dropped us at night in the middle of the bush and we had to find our way home," says Luhrmann. "It was terrifying."

Despite being "tough, tough, tough," the director maintains his father was fair and that "his obsession was the education of his three boys in his tiny gas station." His voice cracks when he speaks of Leonard's death from cancer in 1999, and it's clear that Luhrmann has a deep love for him. Still, he grants, "It was obviously a pretty mad upbringing."

That upbringing took a turn for the worse when Baz's mother, Barbara, who had issues of her own that he won't discuss, fled to Sydney when he was twelve, leaving him distraught and abandoned—an emotion he carries with him to this day.

Then, at age fifteen, he ran away, moving to his mother's new home, where he created a new life—first in the strict Christian Brothers school (which later would double as Gatsby's mansion), then as an actor, as the head of a small theater company and as a documentary filmmaker—all while in his teens.

Like Gatsby, he turned his back on the small world that had let him down. And, like Gatsby (formerly James Gatz), he changed his name. In a stunning act of reinvention, he took on a nickname given him at school in a joking reference to the TV character, Basil Brush, whose haircut resembled his own.

Mark was no more; from now on he would be Baz Luhrmann.

With this new identity, Luhrmann propelled himself forward, ferociously driven to succeed. He starred opposite Judy Davis in the 1981 film *The Winter of Our Dreams*, and worked as a bricklayer by day while appearing in the theater at night, before attending Australia's National Institute for Dramatic Art.

After graduation, he turned a short, semi-autobiographical play into the film that would put him on the map. *Strictly Ballroom* wasn't just about a young man striving to break the conventions of ballroom dancing; it was about Baz himself, with a thinly veiled version of his larger-than-life mother played by actress Pat Thomson. (His real-life mother was an extra in *Gatsby* and has appeared in all his films.)

The movie became a worldwide hit in 1992 and got Luhrmann an invitation to Cannes, launching a career that would include 1996's *Romeo + Juliet* and 2001's *Moulin Rouge!*, which divided critics but gained him a best picture Oscar nomination.

By then he was married to Catherine Martin, a fellow Australian and NIDA graduate whom he had met when she interviewed to handle the costumes for *Ballroom*. Martin recalls being distinctly unenthusiastic when she came to the apartment where he lived above a brothel. "I had the incredible arrogance of youth, and I thought, 'What kind of name is Baz, anyway? And all he does is musicals.'" Then they started talking, and "we are still engaged in a conversation about life and art and the world that started over twenty years ago."

By age forty, Luhrmann no longer was a small-town kid but a global celebrity. Then he faltered.

Alexander was a stunning blow. "It was the first time I set out to do something that I could not make happen," he reflects, "and around the same time we were having trouble conceiving children. [They now have a nine-year-old daughter and seven-year-old son.] It was heartbreaking. It was shattering. I was lost."

Then came the disappointment of his 2008 epic *Australia*, which earned $211 million worldwide but was largely dismissed by critics. The *New Yorker*'s David Denby even argued, "Luhrmann is drawn to kitsch as inevitably as a bear to honey."

"It was really a difficult time," admits Luhrmann.

And yet what's intriguing is how he responded. Rather than retreat to his Sydney cocoon, he reached out for something even bolder, as if the survivor instincts his father had drummed in were kicking into high gear.

"I knew when I went out again," he says, "I would see anyone and do anything to make sure *Gatsby* stayed alive."

The idea of filming Fitzgerald's work came to Luhrmann when he listened to it as a book-on-tape while traveling on the Trans-Siberian Express in 2004.

"The train was basically full of Chinese people smuggling stuff into Mongolia," he recalls. "I had two bottles of red wine and the new iPod with two recorded books. There's Siberia ticking by, and the birch trees, and the wine bottle, and I'm listening [to *Gatsby*]—and when it ended, I had inconsolable melancholia. I was like, 'Can we do all that again?'"

After inquiring about the rights, he found that Sony-based producers Doug Wick and Lucy Fisher were closing a deal with A&E, which had made a *Gatsby* TV movie with Mira Sorvino and Tony Stephens in 2000. The two parties agreed to join forces, then Luhrmann approached DiCaprio.

"I was excited, but it is a daunting task to make an adaptation of any novel, let alone one woven into the fabric of America," says DiCaprio. His decades-long friendship with Luhrmann proved decisive. "Baz and I are able to be incredibly honest with each other. You try to do that with every director, but when you have a long friendship with him, you have the capacity to be incredibly direct. I wouldn't have felt so comfortable taking on this material if I didn't have a relationship like that."

The star was soon joined by Tobey Maguire (Nick Carraway) and Joel Edgerton (Tom Buchanan), who replaced Ben Affleck when he dropped out to make *Argo*. Then an intense search got under way for Daisy, Gatsby's lodestone. Luhrmann reportedly considered a host of actresses from Blake Lively to Scarlett Johansson to Natalie Portman to Michelle Williams before auditioning *An Education*'s Carey Mulligan.

"I only found out about it three days before the audition," recalls Mulligan, "so I read the book quickly for the first time and went to see him. It was unlike any audition I had done, in a loft in SoHo, reading with Leo, and there was a huge 3D camera, a handheld camera, and people taking photographs—really like a workshop for the scene."

Mulligan hung on for weeks before learning she had the part. She was at a formal dinner with Martin, who handed her a cell phone. Luhrmann was on the other end to tell her the good news. Mulligan burst into tears.

But it was unclear the movie was a go. With his cast waiting in the wings and locations on hold, Luhrmann discovered Sony was pulling out; miraculously, Warners now agreed to shoulder the burden in partnership with Village Roadshow Pictures.

Now the production shifted from New York to Australia, benefiting from its 40 percent-plus tax breaks. In September 2011, Luhrmann commenced the type of nightmare shoot every director fears when Australia experienced its third-rainiest season ever. "We got washed out three times in the Blue Mountains," recalls producer Fisher. "We drove three times to a location that was a several-hour drive—and every time it was pouring."

The rains weren't the only problem. Out-of-control paparazzi invaded a house rented for DiCaprio, forcing him to seek refuge in a hotel and leading the crew to construct a vinyl screen to block him from photographers. At the same time, camera cranes took on lives of their own, with one nearly crashing into Edgerton and another leaving that gash in Luhrmann's head, requiring four stitches. Worst of all was when the three-hundred-strong crew gathered again in February, only to find a strange, potentially noxious fog belching from the earth, leading safety officers to evacuate the set. "It was a giant circus," remembers Luhrmann. "I got one shot of Leonardo in a military uniform, then we had to pull out."

Now, fifteen months later, Warners seems genuinely convinced it has something special on its hands. Early tracking bodes well, and if the film fulfills its promise it will remind audiences just how unique Luhrmann is in today's film world.

"I don't think I have ever met anybody who has such a visual sense of the world he wants to create," says Sue Kroll, Warners' president of worldwide marketing, who was traveling when Luhrmann came in for his initial meeting but then became a crucial supporter. "He is an incredible artist. I look at this movie and it is sumptuous, it's so gorgeous. He has an unbelievable eye and an incredible sense of how things are communicated. He is very deliberate about everything he does and it all adds up to telling a different kind of story."

Few directors are so willing to go out on a limb; even fewer do so with his peculiar mix of chutzpah and heart. "His primary motor is that of a genuine artist who is compelled to tell his story," says Wick. "He's like an alchemist looking for the right mix, and he is fearless in pursuing it."

Luhrmann has avoided the safety of a franchise, stayed away from anything that ever seems like a sure bet. An inner force keeps pushing him to probe further, ever testing himself, taunting disaster just like those drivers who would sometimes careen off the bridge next to his Herons Creek home.

"For some reason, I am wedded to risk," he admits.

He no longer is the wunderkind who was a legend at drama school and made his first feature in his early twenties. Nearly three decades later, he only has five films behind him (along with a host of theater and opera productions) and is haunted by the sense time might be running out.

He keeps reminding this reporter that he is now fifty, though he looks years younger, and says the prospect of not completing his work drives him unceasingly. He currently is writing a full-length stage adaptation of *Strictly Ballroom* that will debut in Sydney next year and says he is working on a number of other projects, including a potential TV series for

Sony. Like Gatsby, he believes in the green light, that "orgastic future that year by year recedes before us."

"I feel like my time is limited, and I've always felt that," he reflects. "I don't fear dying, but I feel there are things I would still like to get done."

Past Is Present in the New *Gatsby*

Tom Ryan / 2013

An edited version of this interview appeared in the *Australian*, May 31, 2013.
Published by permission of the author.

Research junkie that he is, Baz Luhrmann doesn't do anything by half measures. There have been six screen adaptations of F. Scott Fitzgerald's 1925 novel, *The Great Gatsby*: he's made one himself and seen all there is to see of the others. Even the little-known *G* (2002), a "hip-hop version" which makes no acknowledgement of *Gatsby* in its credits and draws heavily on Fitzgerald's plot, characters, and themes, but also boldly goes its own way.

Set in the Hamptons and preoccupied with the seductive temptations of the lifestyle the region proffers to the unwary, it recasts Gatsby as reclusive rap mogul Summer G. (Richard T. Jones), thoroughbred Tom Buchanan as venal financier Chip Hightower (Blair Underwood), sad, self-absorbed Daisy as his disillusioned wife, Sky (Chenoa Maxwell), and Nick Carraway as idealistic music journalist Tre Hutcherson (Andre Royo). The third feature for African American writer-director Christopher Scott Cherot, it was produced by Andrew Lauren, who reshaped Fitzgerald's story, has a minor role as Summer G.'s personal assistant, and has a famous father, Luhrmann points out to me, named Ralph.

The route it takes is not the one that the Australian filmmaker wanted to follow, asserting his commitment to Fitzgerald's concerns and vision. "In *Romeo + Juliet* we created a world to clarify and amplify the text, you know, just so as we could close the distance [between Shakespeare's setting and now]. Fitzgerald's novel marks the beginning of the modern era and it is such a perfect reflection of who we are that you don't really need to change much. And whether you like our interpretation or not, it's true to the book. All I needed to do was remove some of the distance. Nick Carraway gives a poetic internal description of what's happening around him, but what he's describing isn't quiet. It's called the roaring twenties."

However, with the help of the estimable Shawn "Jay-Z" Carter, Luhrmann has incorporated hip-hop into his *Gatsby* mix. Seamlessly. "When people asked Fitzgerald why he was putting this African American street music called jazz into his book, he told them that it was 'of the moment.' Now, though, it's not as dangerous as that other form of African American music called hip-hop. So I added that, thinking that, as long as I did the translation of the music, the world [of that time would merge neatly with ours]."

If it still existed, it would be fascinating to see the first *Gatsby* film, directed by Herbert Brenon (just after he'd completed the first screen version of *Beau Geste*), and released the year after the publication of the novel. According to Luhrmann's research, it drew heavily on the 1926 theatrical production, which opened at Broadway's Ambassador Theater on February 2, 1926, ran for 112 performances, was directed by George Cukor (still a few years away from his debut as a film director), and written by Owen Davis, who'd won a Pulitzer Prize in 1923 for his play *Icebound*. But all that remains of it now is a one-minute trailer available on YouTube.

When Luhrmann began planning for his *Gatsby*, Leonardo DiCaprio was quickly on board. Then it all started to happen. The director's hunt for a present for his lead actor fortuitously turned out to be more than a mere diversion from the task in hand. "I was trying to get a first-edition copy of the book to give Leonardo discreetly and they told me that an original dust-jacket version cost half a million bucks," he recalls. "I said, 'I don't think I can do that.'" Not one who gives up easily, he kept looking, eventually coming across an edition he could buy for $5000. "I looked inside the cover and it was signed by a Herbert Brenon to Warner Baxter, saying 'You're the best Great Gatsby.' I went, hang on, Warner Baxter?! A silent film? I didn't know about that. So I looked everywhere for it. I even checked out Mosfilm [in Moscow, the largest studio/archive in Europe]." Without luck. "I only know that Fitzgerald walked out of it and that both it and the subsequent one are based on a play that he had nothing to do with."

Almost a decade after the novelist's death, expatriate Australian John Farrow was set to direct the second adaptation of *The Great Gatsby* (1949), with Tyrone Power and Gene Tierney. But then Farrow exited the project, citing "creative differences," followed by his leads. Elliott Nugent took over the helm and Alan Ladd stepped into the title role, bringing with him the intriguing mix of placidity and noirish danger that defines his screen persona. Unfortunately, the censors also left their fingerprints on the film, insisting that audiences needed to know up front that Gatsby is an unsavoury type. As a result, an early montage finds him locked inside an iconic night-time gangster-movie scene, shooting out of the window of a speeding car.

"This one is, to me, an amusing curioso," says Luhrmann of Nugent's film, which is now hard to track down. "It doesn't entirely work, but it's got some great vignettes in it that I adore. There's this early scene where Alan Ladd walks into his mansion and says, 'Yeah, I really like the place here,' and proceeds to explain how he wants it to look. 'I'll have some rugs here . . .' and so on. What I really liked about the scene was the way it establishes Gatsby as a fantasist, that he was decorating his own building. And that was an interesting cue."

"There are two other things about the film that I really like. First of all, if you want to do a wild, crazy party, always put a white horse into it. It's de rigueur, and they have a white horse walking through a lounge room. But the thing I love the most is the scene where Reba [Jack Lambert], an old acquaintance, turns up at the party. And he says [Luhrmann pursing his lips, punk-style, and putting on a tough-guy gangster voice with a tinge of the James Cagneys], 'Your name's . . . your name's not Jake Gatsby. You're Jimmy Gatz.' Right away, Ladd says, 'Could I speak to you for a moment?' And then he takes him to a private spot and BAM. I toyed with the idea, but it became a case of me enjoying myself and not really serving the text."

What's fascinating about the next *Gatsby* adaptation, the much-maligned 1974 version, scripted by Francis Ford Coppola, directed by Englishman Jack Clayton (*The Pumpkin Eater*, *The Innocents*), and starring Robert Redford and Mia Farrow (and Sam Waterston as the most dignified of all the screen Nicks), is how much it has in common with Luhrmann's version, even though it's also a very different film. The similarities are numerous: Gatsby's first appearance occurs about thirty minutes into both films (whose running-time is the same: 143 minutes); he's played in each by a handsome heartthrob; a minor variation on the art deco "JG" monogram that appears in passing in the earlier film pervades Luhrmann's; both adopt a compare-and-contrast approach to the various sexual relationships in the story; and, perhaps most important of all, the visual emphases in each of them assert that the characters are owned by the wealth piled up around them rather than the other way around.

But whereas Clayton's film, shot by the brilliant Douglas Slocombe (whose credits range from Joseph Losey's *The Servant* to two of Steven Spielberg's *Raiders* films), primarily surveys the plush settings and décor in a detached, dispassionate fashion, Luhrmann's version, shot by New Zealander Simon Duggan, immerses us inside its 3D world. Close-ups and framings insist on the dominance of material objects over the characters' existence at the same time as Gatsby, Daisy, and Nick, for all their flaws, search for something transcendent, something to take them out of themselves.

Luhrmann acknowledges that seeing the 1974 version at "the little cinema at Laurieton" run by his father was what first set him in pursuit of Gatsby. "I thought that Robert Redford was the coolest man in the world," he remembers. "By the time I saw *Gatsby*, I would have been twelve. I remember seeing it and thinking it was beautiful but 'who the hell is that guy?' I did not understand it at all. The book was required reading at school, but I don't know if I read it at the time. But ten years ago, I was on the Trans-Siberian train on my way to see my wife . . . you probably read that story."

I had: it's the one about his rediscovering *Gatsby* as an audio book. "I put it on and thought, 'Fuck. I didn't know that book at all.' It was such a great reflection of the era. And I was blown away by the technique of it: it's a novella not a novel, and novellas do make good movies. So I thought that if I could unlock the voice of Nick Carraway, there was a cinematic treatment of it that I could do." The encounter on the train then led him back to Fitzgerald's prose on the page, not just to *Gatsby*, but to everything he wrote and, it seems, everything others have written about him.

"I went back to the Redford, of course," he continues. "I thought it was very interesting, and I was very lucky. There's a screenplay for it written by Truman Capote, which I got my hands on. Bob Evans, whom I now know very well and who was running the studio at the time, rejected it. Because, basically, Jordan is gay and Nick is gay and the script is too hardcore. Truman was really upset about it and went on television and called Paramount a bunch of wankers. It's in his hand, but it's totally legible. It's also unfinished. Basically, it's mad and bad and crazy."

But, he concedes, Capote might have been on to something. It's an idea which TV veteran Robert Markowitz's *Gatsby* telemovie, made in 2000 and written by John J. McLaughlin (*Black Swan*, *Hitchcock*), toys with as well, evocatively suggesting an undeclared homoerotic connection between Nick and Gatsby (played by Paul Rudd and Robert

Stephens). For Luhrmann, Nick's breakdown is crucial to such a reading: "He's writing the book about Gatsby because he's trying to work out his feelings towards him which, in any interpretation, are deeply romantic."

"So, are they physically romantic? I don't think they ever were in the story. But is it possible that Nick Carraway could ever be physically romantic with a man? All that is going to be answered after the book is completed, when Nick Carraway is ready to be Nick Carraway, when he's been able to find himself.

"The whole point is: he is within and he is without. He watches himself and he's in it. The book is so deft at that."

"Now if you want my own take, and this will blow your mind, if you haven't read it already. *Absolution* [a Fitzgerald short story first published in 1924] is spoken about as one of the primary references for *Gatsby* and it's about a sort of 'mystical' experience that a young man has with a priest, with a lot of sweating and smoke in the room. Go figure." Luhrmann goes on to suggest that there might also be more to Gatsby's back story about sailing the world with the elderly yachtsman, Dan Cody, than actually appears on the pages of Fitzgerald's novel.

There are no hints of the kind in Luhrmann's film, however. And, he continues, it's "the genius" of Fitzgerald's novel, and an earlier galley of it, entitled *Trimalchio*, that primarily drove his thinking about his Gatsby. "We'd been working closely with Professor James West for two years," he explains. "He's edited an edition of *Trimalchio*. When it reached Max Perkins [Fitzgerald's editor at Scribner's], Perkins basically implied that he thought it was boring because you didn't know who Gatsby was until the end. So Scott, who's in the South of France, takes the 'I've essentially been Pygmalion-ed by Dan Cody' stuff and puts it right in the middle of the book, straight after the lovers get back together again. To me, that's what makes *Trimalchio* a lovely book and is one of the things that makes the structure of the book gay . . . gay!? Hrmph! [shaking his head at himself, then correcting his misspeak] . . . great. Probably a bit gay too."

While working with longtime collaborator Craig Pearce on the screenplay, Luhrmann explains, he looked carefully at how the other films presented the information about Gatsby's time with Cody. "In the Alan Ladd, they keep that in, in an interesting way, and they throw a lot of weight on Ella Kaye [Cody's mistress who, in Nugent's film, throws herself at Gatsby immediately after Cody's death].

"One fascinating thing we came across in our research that you won't know . . . Well, you might know, but I've never told anyone. There's a penny-dreadful book called *Filming "The Great Gatsby"* by Bruce

Bahrenburg, a journalist who spent a year on the set of the 1974 film. It's clear from it that a lot of the hassles I had, they did too: they had to shoot most of it in England, problems with unions, the weather, the whole nine yards. . . . But this is the revelation: there's a scene, which Bahrenburg describes in the book, where he gets to be with Redford, a bit like you're with me now, and Redford's in the middle of shooting and obsessed about putting the Dan Cody story into the middle of the movie. He thinks that it's extremely important to reveal who Gatsby is just as the lovers are getting back together again."

"He said he wanted it like the book. So that's what we did. Just as the lovers get back together, boom, you get some dirt. So when Tom Buchanan's coming over to sniff it out, you're going, 'This isn't good.' And Gatsby's about to tell Daisy that she should leave her husband! No wonder Nick goes, 'Wait, wait, wait. You think she's gonna leave a Kennedy who lives in that building over there and move across to Disneyland?' She's living in 1922 with all the social mores of the time. 'You're crazy.' He doesn't say those words. What he does say is 'You can't repeat the past.' Gatsby says, 'Of course, you can.' And that way lies madness, my friend."

"Redford was on to it. He knew that you have to reveal Gatsby's back story right in the middle of the movie. And when we went to do that, there was a lot of 'Should we do that? That's against cinematic form.' But whether you like our interpretation or not, it's true to the book. The stakes go up at that point."

"What I think is interesting—and no one's ever written about it, no one knows—is that Redford instinctively knew it was right and the director didn't do it."

Luhrmann was determined not to make the same mistake.

And he also took another key lesson from his *Gatsby* predecessor, to do with how his team was going to approach the marketing of the film. "Bob Evans warned us to watch out about this," he explains, doing an Evans imitation (or at least that's what I think it was). "He brought out a *Time* magazine cover about the hype involved in the selling of Paramount's *The Great Gatsby*. He said, 'You don't want pots and pans. We had pots and pans. And a very beautiful and very boring movie.'"

"Everybody wanted to be involved commercially with our film," Luhrmann notes, "but we only said yes to partners—that's what we called them—who had a specific relationship with Fitzgerald. He was a customer at Tiffany's, for example. In the period, they made pearls like those that Tom Buchanan gives Daisy as a rites-of-passage gift. So my wife [co-producer, production, and costume designer Catherine Martin] worked very hard with their archives to get the detail right. And in Fitzgerald's first novel, *The Far Side of Paradise*, a character is advised to go to Brooks Brothers to get himself a nice suit. They had letters from Fitzgerald . . . all of these old houses have great archives. We needed a lot of suits, so we went to Brooks Brothers. They had the milling, the fabric, all of that."

Hardly a pots and pans approach. And, given box office success the film has achieved despite the mixed reviews it has received and audiences' sustained reservations about 3D—Luhrmann noting the reluctance of young women at the film's Australian premiere in Sydney last week to wear 3D glasses because they would mark their make-up—it would seem to be working.

Appendix: Notes from John Duigan and Geoffrey Nottage

The following excerpts are from interviews conducted by the editor during his research into the early period of Luhrmann's career. Reprinted by permission.

Writer-director John Duigan looks back on working with Luhrmann on *Winter of Our Dreams*

Baz was, I think, just seventeen when he came in to read for *Winter of Our Dreams*, slightly disheveled, very boyish looking. As I remember it, he had just arrived in Sydney from somewhere in the remote outback, though reading his biog I see he had spent some of his schooling in the city's suburbs. I was surprised that someone from a remote country town seemed so self-confident, though it was not in a cocky way.

The character of Pete was a street-smart kid with a tough exterior but vulnerable underneath. He had three important scenes with Lou, the female lead, a damaged prostitute with a heroin addiction, to be played by Judy Davis. Baz understood Pete's skin-deep bravado, and read well in his audition.

At the time, Judy was the emerging young star of the Australian film scene, having recently, and memorably, played the lead in Gillian Armstrong's fine film *My Brilliant Career*. Judy had already acquired a fledgling reputation as, on occasions, being a touch moody and difficult—in those days, in my experience, she simply didn't suffer fools gladly.

I try to get as much rehearsal as I can on all my films, but in this case I also saw it as an opportunity to break the ice between Judy and Baz in case he was nervous acting with an already established star. I needn't have worried as it turned out. Conscious of Baz's inexperience, Judy was very generous in her working with him. For his part, Baz was an enthusiast, and his enthusiasm was infectious: he loved the process of rehearsing, filming, and bringing the scenes to life. I had the impression he thoroughly enjoyed the whole experience, and I was very happy with their scenes together. Both characters are desperately in need of a friend, but are already too defended to reveal this to one another. Pete has a crush on the much older Lou, which she indulges without patronizing him. But she swats him away when he tries anything too intimate. The scenes are funny and touching.

A few years later, I was casting the miniseries *Vietnam*, with Chris Noonan and Terry Hayes, and suggested we earmark Baz for the role of the then eighteen-year-old Nicole Kidman's boyfriend—at the time, he was just finishing his course at NIDA, and was unknown to them. When he finally came in to audition, I was dismayed to find his acting had, it seemed to me, rather lost its natural spontaneity, and become somewhat affected. As a result, we ended up casting John Polson in the role. He, co-incidentally, also went on subsequently to find success as a film director.

I am sure if Baz had pursued acting as a career, he would have soon re-connected with the vital spark I had seen in *Winter*—at that time, I thought he had every chance of developing into a fine leading man. As it transpired, that spark ignited in a quite different direction, and, ironically, he ended up years later directing Nicole in *Moulin Rouge* and *Australia*, and Judy as Elsa Schiaparelli in the *Elsa Schiaparelli and Miuccia Prada: Impossible Conversations* short films for the Met.

(Correspondence dated August 25, 2012)

Director Geoffrey Nottage on working with Baz Luhrmann on the filming of *La Boheme*

At the beginning of 1993, Greg Shears, the executive producer at the Australian Broadcasting Commission's TV Arts & Entertainment, approached me about directing the TV coverage of Baz Luhrmann and Catherine Martin's wildly beautiful and stunningly successful Australian Opera production that had overflowed seats at its first outing twelve months earlier.

The AO had pushed for Baz to direct the nine-camera production, but Greg had flatly refused this, pointing out that this sort of production, especially under "live" conditions, was a specialized area of directing.

When I came aboard, I had a feeling before the first meeting with Baz at the Opera House, that both parties to the deal, ABC and AO, were waiting to see how Baz and I got along—or more precisely, I suspect, how Baz reacted to me.

At the meeting, I was at pains to tell him that I was there solely to put his production on to video, not to create my own. I don't remember too many details of that meeting but I left thinking that it went alright, and that Baz was OK. During the camera planning stages and the general pre-production period, I can't remember ever seeing Baz. But on the night of the first recording—generally viewed as a "shake-out" session—I was told that Baz was sitting in the second Outside Broadcast van, watching it all unfold with an eagle-eyed intensity. Baz's desire to understand this style and genre of recording was palpable. He never once approached me with demands or suggestions, and I appreciated that.

Baz's contribution to the video process was to organize two, three-hour calls with the entire cast over two days, with the singers miming to the final recording. I don't believe that had ever happened before, or has ever happened since, and it's testament to his almost uncanny skills at persuasion. His main aim was to re-light and re-shoot Mimi's first entrance. He wanted the audience to have the same reaction as Rodolfo to the beauty and romance of the face.

I never heard what Baz thought about the finished product. But I enjoyed the brief working relationship we had. I found him committed and thoughtful, but never demanding. He seemed to believe what I had said on that first day about putting his vision on the screen. It remains one of my happiest and most rewarding experiences.

(Correspondence dated June 20, 2013)

Additional Resources

Adamek, Pauline. "*Romeo and Juliet*: Interview with Baz Luhrmann." *POP-film*, November 3, 1996 [Q&A source for the *Cinema Papers* interview feature included herein].

Andrew, Geoff. "Baz Luhrmann." *The Guardian*, September 7, 2001.

Bauer, Erik. "Re-revealing Shakespeare: An Interview with Baz Luhrmann." *Creative Screenwriting* 5, no. 2 (1998).

Bierly, Mandi. "Baz Luhrmann Exclusive: The Director Talks *Strictly Ballroom* and Whether He'll Ever Direct an Episode of *Glee*." *Entertainment Weekly*, December 8, 2010.

Binkley, Christina. "Speakeasy: Judy Davis Plays Elsa Schiaparelli in Baz Luhrmann Film." *Wall Street Journal*, April 26, 2012.

Bodey, Michael. "Global Take on Outback." *The Australian*, December 29, 2007.

Brealey, Louise. "Strictly Luhrmann," *Premiere* (UK), April 1, 1997.

Camilotti, Camila Paula. "Shakespeare's *Romeo and Juliet* Beyond the Boundaries of Page: An Analysis of Baz Luhrmann's *Romeo + Juliet* and Its Balcony Scene." *Academic Journal of Interdisciplinary Studies* 2, no. 4 (2013).

Caplan, Nina. "Baz Luhrmann on *Australia*." *Time Out* (UK).

Cochrane, Peter. "Baz Finds His Place in the Sun." *Sydney Morning Herald*, December 23, 1996.

Conor, Liz. "A 'Nation So Ill-Begotten': Racialized Childhood and Conceptions of National Belonging in Xavier Herbert's *Poor Fellow My Country* and Baz Luhrmann's *Australia*." *Studies in Australasian Cinema* 4, no. 2 (2010).

Cook, Pam. *Baz Luhrmann*. World Directors series, BFI/Palgrave Macmillan, London, 2010. See also http://www.bfi.org.uk/filmtvinfo/researchers/tales/cook.html; http://fashionintofilm.wordpress.com/2012/03/05/the-curtain-lifted-baz-luhrmann-cm-and-me/ [dealing with her visit to the House of Iona]; and http://www.sensesofcinema.com/2011/book-reviews/baz-luhrmann-by-pam-cook/.

Cieply, Michael. "The Rich Are Different: They're in 3-D." *New York Times*, January 17, 2012.

Danielsen, Shane. "Something for Everyone." *The Australian*, December 10, 1997.

Davis, Erik. "*Australia* Director: Baz Luhrmann." *Cinematical*, March 4, 2009.

D'Erasmo, Stacey. "The Look of Love." *New York Times Magazine*, November 3, 2002.

Downing, Crystal. "Misshapen Chaos of Well-Seeming Form: Baz Luhrmann's *Romeo + Juliet*." *Literature/Film Quarterly* 28, no. 2 (2000).

Fischer, Paul. "Interview: Baz Luhrmann." *Moviehole*, November 24, 2008.

Fox, Killian. "How We Made the Epic of Oz." *The Guardian*, November 2, 2008.

Frank, Jason. "Interview: Baz Luhrmann, Director." Games First!, April 16, 2002. http://www.gamesfirst.com/articles/jfrank/baz_inter view/baz_interview.htm.

Freeman-Greene, Suzy. "Bold as Baz." *The Age* (Melbourne), January 15, 1994.

Fuller, Graham, "Strictly Red." *Sight and Sound*, June 2001.

Galloway, Stephen. "Baz Luhrmann Readies His Greek Epic." *The Hollywood Reporter*, October 1, 2002.

Galloway, Stephen. "Baz Luhrmann's Despair, Drive and Gamble Behind *Great Gatsby*." *The Hollywood Reporter*, April 24, 2013.

Gray, Simon. "Thunder Down Under." *American Cinematographer*, November 2008 [on the collaboration with cinematographer Mandy Walker].

Green, Jesse. "How Do You Make a Movie Sing?" *New York Times*, May 13, 2001.

Greer, Germaine. "Strictly Fanciful." *The Age*, December 17, 2008.

Hamilton, Lucy. "Baz vs. the Bardolaters, Or Why *William Shakespeare's Romeo + Juliet* Deserves Another Look." *Literature-Film Quarterly* 28, no. 2 (2000).

Healy, Patrick. "Artsbeat: Luhrmann Heads Towards Broadway." *New York Times*, September 24, 2010.

Horn, John. "Baz Luhrmann Wants to 'Reveal' More of *The Great Gatsby*." *Los Angeles Times*, April 26, 2013.

Horton, Robert. "*Strictly Ballroom*." *Film Comment*, January–February 1993.

Jackman, Christine. "The Movie Magician." *The Australian*, November 1, 2008.

Jayamanne, Laleen. "The Drover's Wives and Camp Couture: Baz Luhrmann's Preposterous National Epic." *Studies in Australasian Cinema* 4, no. 2 (2010).

Jenkins, David. "The Dionysus of Down Under." *The Sunday Age* (Melbourne), November 19, 2000.

Jenson, Jeff. "First Tango in Paris." *Entertainment Weekly*, May 25, 2001.

Jones, Kent. "Real Artifice: *Moulin Rouge*." *Film Comment*, May–June, 2001.

Kelly, Richard T. "Interview with Baz Luhrmann." *The Great Gatsby: Official Film Edition*, Picador.

Loehlin, James N. "'These Violent Delights Have Violent Ends': Baz Luhrmann's Millennial Shakespeare." In *Shakespeare, Film, Fin De Siécle*, edited by Mark T. Burnett and Ramona Wray. New York: St. Martin's, 2000.

Luhrmann, Baz. "Act 1: The Nation Struggles to Find Its Voice." *The Age*, November 5, 1999.

———. "Australia and America: A Shared Hope and Changed Attitude." *Huffington Post*, January 14, 2009.

———. "Baz Luhrmann on Reimagining *The Great Gatsby*." Stylist, stylist.co.uk, 2013.

———. Director's Notes (on directing *La Boheme* on Broadway). Featured on the opening night on Broadway playbill.

———. "George Sidney." *Directors Guild of America Magazine*, July 2002.

———. "How Has Hollywood Changed?" *Hollywood Reporter, International Edition*, December 3, 2001.

———. "Kylie and Puccini." *Sunday Times*, September 9, 2001.

———. *Moulin Rouge! A Film Directed by Baz Luhrmann*. Crows Nest, Australia: Allen & Unwin, 2001.

———. "On Chaplin." *Sight & Sound*, October 2003.

———. "On Preston Sturges." *Sight & Sound*, May 2000.

———. "What Now? A New Perspective on Australian Film." *Lumina* (Australian Film Television and Radio School), no. 1.

———. "With Nicole Kidman." *Interview*, May 2001.

Luhrmann, Baz, and Craig Pearce. *Romeo + Juliet*. London: Hodder Children's Books, 1997 [screenplay].

———. *Strictly Ballroom*. Sydney: Currency Press, 1992 [screenplay and short articles].

McFarlane, Brian. "*Strictly Ballroom*: Old Story, New Images." *mETAphor*, Issue 3, July, 2000.

McFarlane, Brian. "There's a Lot Going On in *Australia*." *Metro* (Australia), no. 159.

Michod, David. "*Moulin Rouge!*: The Co-Writer." *if MAG*, May 2001 [on the collaboration with Craig Pearce].

Myers, Eric. "Strictly Bohemian: Eric Myers Talks to Baz Luhrmann." *Opera News*, March 1, 2003.

Moodie, Ann-Maree. *Local Heroes*. Prentice Hall Australia, 1996.

Papson, Stephen. "Baz Luhrmann's *Australia*: When Excess Isn't Parody." *Jump Cut*, no. 53 (Summer 2011).

Pride, Ray. "Bright Angels: Ray Pride Talks to Baz Luhrmann about His Impassioned *Romeo + Juliet*." *Newcity* (Chicago), November 1996.

Quinn, Karl. "Drag, Dags and the Suburban Surreal." *Metro* (Australia), no. 100 (Summer 1994–95).

Rattigan, Neil. *Strictly Ballroom: A Film for Our Time*. University of New England, Armidale, NSW, 2005.

Rochlin, Margy. "Think Bollywood, Australia and Paris in Song." *New York Times*, May 6, 2001.

Salvador, Olga Seco. "*Strictly Ballroom* (1992): Departure from Traditional Anglo-Australian Discourses or Veiled Confirmation of Old National-Encouragement Mechanisms?" *Miscelanea: A Journal of English and American Studies* 32 (2005).

Schembri, Jim. "Why Baz Did the Bard." *The Age* (Melbourne), December 24, 1996.

Talati-Parikh, Sitanshi. "Amplifying Emotion." *VerveOnline* 18, issue 3, March, 2010.

Taylor, Ronnie. "Baz Luhrmann's *Strictly Ballroom*." *Cinema Papers*, no. 88, May–June, 1992.

Walker, Elsie. "Pop Goes the Shakespeare: Baz Luhrmann's *Romeo + Juliet*." *Literature/Film Quarterly* 28, no. 2 (2000).

Warne-Smith, Drewe. "Scene Stealer." *The Australian*, December 1, 2007 [on the collaboration with Catherine Martin].

Welsh, Jim. "Postmodern Shakespeare: Strictly Romeo." *Literature/Film Quarterly* 25, no. 2, 1997.

West, James L. "What Baz Luhrmann Asked Me about *The Great Gatsby*." *Moviefone*, April 10, 2008.

Index

Printed in Great Britain
by Amazon

87043920R00109